Advance Praise for

"What a pleasure it has been for Th
recent events featuring Steffany Bart
in" medium, but a beautiful presence, ...
presenter, and a warm, caring person. Before she even gets started
amazing people with her accuracy, she connects with her audience
in a way which inspires them to lay aside skepticism and open to the
wonders of God's Universe. We all look forward to the next time!"

— *REV. PHYLIS CLAY SPARKS*, Spiritual Director of
The Soul-Esteem Center, St. Louis, Missouri

"Yesterday, at the Afterlife Awareness conference in Portland, I saw
an angel. Pretty neat, huh? Her name is Steffany Barton and she lives
in Kansas. She's a medium who specializes in contacting suicides. If
central casting were to deliver an actress to hover over the manger in
Bethlehem, Steffany would fit the bill to a tee. She's lovely, luminous,
and full of grace."

— *DAVID CHILSTROM*, Afterlife Awareness Conference Reporter,
Portland, OR

"Steffany's wisdom helps those touched by suicide to embrace a deeper
understanding of the soul. She breaks down the fear-based religious
beliefs, myths and misconceptions that can often inhibit healing, and
offers readers a new understanding of the soul's journey. This book
is easy to read, uplifting, encouraging and comforting to anybody,
regardless of their spiritual outlook."

— *TERRI DANIEL*, President and Founder, The Afterlife Conference

"Steffany Barton has provided a masterful, life-changing book on a
difficult subject, fulfilling her stated desire to soothe the wounded heart
and welcome a sense of peace. It speaks to the heart with a wisdom
beyond words."

— *JIM PATHFINDER EWING*, author of *Redefining Manhood: A Guide for
Men and Those Who Love Them*

FACING DARKNESS, FINDING LIGHT

Life After Suicide

Healing comfort for those left behind

Steffany Barton, RN

FINDHORN PRESS

Published in 2016 by Findhorn Press, Scotland

ISBN 978-1-84409-688-6

Edited by Nicky Leach
Cover by Richard Crookes
Interior design by Damian Keenan
Printed and bound in the USA

Published by
Findhorn Press
117-121 High Street,
Forres IV36 1AB,
Scotland, UK

t +44 (0)1309 690582
f +44 (0)131 777 2711
e info@findhornpress.com
www.findhornpress.com

Contents

Author's Note 9

Introduction – Losing Julie 15

1   End to Begin 22
2   Awake and Alive 34
3   Been There, Done With That 43
4   Showing Up 52
5   Look Again, See Anew 60
6   From Darkness Here to Light There 69
7   Why This? 77
8   Faultless 87
9   Forgive to Remember 97
10   Floating Boats and Driftwood 107
11   Bridging The Gap 117
12   After the Rain 125

Dedication

For my husband David:
You taught me to trust the still, soft voices
and to listen to silence behind the noises.
I love you.

Author's Note

I am a mother. I am trained and licensed as a registered nurse. I am a wife and a writer and a public speaker. I am a daughter who has lost her mother and a friend who is bereaved. I am a person, not much different from anyone who will read these words, who is making the most of what I've got.

And what I've got is a deep sense of compassion for those who have experienced loss. I have a profound sensitivity to the emotional impact that death has, and I have a strong desire to bring into words the unexpressed emotions that survivors of suicide may have in the days and years that follow such a traumatic loss.

Part of who I am, beyond my professional degree and college education, is a spiritual student and teacher. I know that we are more than atoms and molecules; we are energy in motion, light that expresses freely. Since energy cannot be destroyed, only changed, I have come to understand that when a body is destroyed, the energy contained within simply changes. It does not end.

Those who commit suicide have a spirit, an energy, that is still somehow, somewhere expressed. And, although I can sense this energy, much like a wine taster can discern subtle notes and nuances in a glass of fine wine, my desire in writing this book is to speak to those still living, or perhaps more truly, those struggling, scraping by, existing, with the pain and perpetual grief of a death by suicide.

I do not believe that suicide is a fate cast, a destiny inevitable. Nor do I believe that we are powerless to intervene when a suicide wish is expressed. On the contrary, I believe that every one of us has the ability to choose our fate and to alter our destiny. Even after a death by suicide, and perhaps especially after this kind of loss, we can, with a willingness of heart and an openness of mind, find a new outlook on life and a gentle way to sooth the wounded heart and welcome a sense of peace.

Suicide is violent and unkind to those left behind. We as a culture shy away from death because it is uncomfortable; talking about suicide is practically taboo. But those who are left behind desperately need to be accepted, heard, and understood if we are to create a cultural climate where suicide can be prevented.

Suicide has become a shameful and silent epidemic. According to the CDC, in 2010 suicide ranked as the 10th leading cause of death in Americans; one person dies through self-inflicted means every 13 minutes. Additionally, the incidence of suicide has increased by 1.7 percent over the last decade. These numbers are high—far too high. Something is missing. We pay lip service to suicide prevention, offer therapy and emergency intervention, but the numbers still rise. Can suicide be prevented?

Yes.

And no.

Suicide prevention begins at birth. We embrace all children as gifts to our planet, as welcomed guests in our lives. We embody gentleness toward our Earth; we grow our patience with each other and ourselves. We teach our children that life is a journey, a vast undertaking and an epic task that is completed, and can only be taken, one small step at a time. We value silence because silence is valuable. We honor cycles and seasons because there is wisdom and rhythm in the ongoing cycles of nature and the ever-changing seasons of life. We embrace our fragility, our strength, our triumphs, and our vulnerability. We show our children that it is ordinary to struggle but extraordinary to find a way to overcome. We laugh when we feel the urge, and we cry to let go. We teach these things because we are willing to live according to our personal truth. When we accept who we are, when we come to life willing to weather the storms, to see past the darkness and into the dawn, we have the power to turn the tides on the frightening trend of suicide.

And yet, I believe that anyone who is touched by death can learn about life. Death reminds us to take nothing for granted. Death offers us a chance to take inventory of our own lives, to be honest about where we are on our own journey, to redefine our goals, our priorities, to be true to who we are.

Those who are left behind after a death by suicide are challenged to find a profound level of courage and faith as they learn to accept that they are guiltless in the suicide and not to blame for the death of another. For many who are left behind, death invites a more spiritual approach to life, a willingness to see beyond that which is measurable fact and into the world of emotion, spirit, and soul.

When is suicide not preventable? If suicide has occurred. As we take this journey through this book, I want to bring to light a singular truth: those who commit suicide could not have been stopped, or the suicide would not have occurred.

A suicide that is committed is a suicide that could not have been prevented. In accepting this, guilt shall be washed away, those survivors, imprisoned by shame, shall once and for all be set free.

Do those who commit suicide experience some sort of disappointment on the other side? Impossible. But those souls, when it's all said and done, often feel a lack of satisfaction with the experience of life, reflecting back, feeling hungry for a second chance, wishing for more.

Yet I believe, and will explore through the book, that when the survivors left behind are able to embrace those who commit suicide for the truth of who they are, peace and healing can begin.

It is not appropriate to think of those loved ones on the other side as perfect angelic beings, nor is it right to think of them in a negative light. As we journey together through this book, I will explore the process of understanding that there is good and bad, love and fear, triumphs and struggles, easy times and hard times that each one of us go through, that there is no "perfect" life, and that we never stop learning and growing and changing. We can truly put to rest the guilt, shame, and fear of death and bring to light a celebration of life!

My goal is to help the bereaved find a voice and to explore tools for healing through understanding the process of living. This means accepting our emotions, choosing to be proactive and responsible in our spiritual growth, learning to be self-aware and willing to give self-care.

Suicide is not an inevitable fate. But in the event of these circumstances of death, there can be a new way to find hope and to experience life for those left behind.

This is a book about finding new life. The path may not always be smooth; the waters might not be crystal clear. Answers rarely come neatly packaged, wrapped up in a tidy box. But this is a journey worth taking. Life is a gift—a fragile, strong treasure. We must handle all of life, everyone, everywhere, with gentle love and the greatest of care.

We will face the darkness together, and we will find light.

If you are considering suicide, or if you are struggling with depression, you might find thoughts of an eternal paradise tempting. Hearing of respite, healing, and complete, deep rest may sound rather alluring. When the pain is too heavy, when the sadness so profound, when the only way through it is to get out of it, death may seem a viable option. Or the only option.

But this is a book about living life!

If you are considering suicide, consider this: cake.

You see, we humans, despite our many foibles and flaws, regardless of our rushing and pushing and running around, want to feel satisfied. We want to know we have succeeded, we want a sense of accomplishment, completion, culmination, pride. Each of us wants to know that we have, in small ways or large, made a difference to someone, anyone, somewhere, anywhere along the line.

Consider cake.

If you've got a yen for some dessert-time Zen, add some icing or some cherries, frosting, cream, fresh strawberries, or just go fresh baked. Cake.

But if you take a cake from the oven too soon, it tastes mushy. Oh, you'll get a quick, soupy sugar fix, and it might be good enough, but it's not fully baked; it's not fully cake. You may be feel let down, a bit disappointed, dissatisfied.

If you wait, anticipate, think about how nice it will taste, be patient, stay steady, hold the line... oh, how sweet it is! The moment all the contents have blended together, when the chemical reaction reaches ravishing perfection, you will find such delicious satisfaction. The delicate aroma, the lovely sight, the soft, warm meltiness of the fluffy confection appeases, makes waiting worthwhile. The simple pleasure and sweet satisfaction of a fresh-baked cake is sublime, divine!

Life gets messy. Like the dirty dishes and the kitchen, sometimes there's clean up required.

Life gets tedious, cumbersome, tiresome, tough. And, unlike cake, life doesn't come with a taste-tested, tried-and-true recipe card. There's no box top to follow, no mix to stir, no instruction card to save for future reference.

Yet you have the ingredients on hand, or at least in your heart, to find peace and to feel soul satisfaction. You might have to fumble around. You may need to stop for a while. You might even want to toss the whole thing out... but, oh, so rich the journey, so sweet the results.

If you're considering suicide, consider this:

You make a difference. You're capable of feeling better. You're able to make a change for your own good. You might not think it, but you're smart. You might not feel it, but you're strong. You might not believe it, but you did not come here to suffer, to hurt, to have what you don't want.

You came here to find satisfaction. You came here to find purpose. You came here for life!

If you are considering suicide, seek help from a professional. Call someone who can work with you. In an emergency, call 911. Get help, ask for support, speak up.

If you're considering suicide, consider this: Death may be an escape, but death cannot satisfy your soul. You did not come here to struggle into nonexistence, to languish and die. You came here to live, to feel satisfied.

And this is YOUR book—a book about life.

Introduction –
Losing Julie

I COULD NOT WAIT. I had to see her. Despite the imminent ho-ho-holiday, with upcoming, out-of-town travel, three kids for whom to play Santa, a presentation to deliver, a newsletter to circulate, and a festooned house long overdue for clean, I put on hold the hustle and bustle and headed to her home.

I could not wait. I wanted to see her.

Julie came to me quite by accident but for a higher purpose. Although I had known of her for nearly a decade, I never met her face to face until one crisp November afternoon, when she rang my door bell. I knew it was her only because, moments before her arrival, I received a text from the babysitter, *"Can't make it today. Sending a sub… Julie. You'll luv her. Thx."*

Opening the door, I took in the unexpected guest. She appeared younger than me, with a full face and ruddy cheeks. Her jawline looked somewhat heavy because of her blunt, bobbed haircut colored in a deep red to orange. Cloaking her upper body was an open woolen sweater of various colors in a pattern that reminded me of the American Southwest. I noticed that, although she had no children, she wore a white turtleneck sweater tucked tightly into her "mom" jeans, which seemed oddly paired with her knee-high, black, military style boots. She looked at me with a twinkling eye paired with a mercurial smile and said, in an alto voice, "Hi. I'm Julie. I'm babysitting your kids."

Motioning her in, I wondered how this would unfold. All considerations were cut short, however, as my children, delighted with a new visitor to entertain, began sharing stories and chatting it up with her like she was an old friend. She laughed, listened, and looked fairly relaxed, so I, too, eased into the moment. This would be fine. Julie seemed okay.

But Julie was not okay. Julie was terminally ill, and dying a slow, painful death. No test could indicate it, and no lab values were off, but she was dis-eased, distressed, depressed, and done with an existence that seemed marked by a string of misspent opportunities and relationships gone horribly wrong. Julie wanted out. She had hurt too badly for far too long.

Still, she held on.

For three consecutive afternoons, Julie appeared on my front porch as the special "guest babysitter." In those hours spent with her, my children and I grew to love the woman. Her devotion to animals won over the heart of my son: she fearlessly reached into our terrarium and gleefully allowed five fire-bellied toads free rein of her arms, trunk, neck, and face. She sculpted a tea set of playdough, crafted a duct tape wallet, read aloud from *King Arthur,* and learned how to properly dress a Barbie doll. She colored her nails, and the kids' nails, too, with permanent marker, and she applied some rub-on tattoos. She loved to draw and made a picture of a singing and dancing cat that filled my eldest daughter with delight.

As my work week ended, we all agreed that her career as a babysitter was a resounding success, and we decided to call upon her in the future, should the need arise.

I handed Julie a check for the week's pay. She looked at me— seemed to look into me— then, breathing , she asked, "Steffany, will you help me?"

"Of course. You know I will. Helping is what I do best," I replied cheerily.

I did not expect what happened next.

"I don't know that I want to be here anymore, you know?" She said, looking at the ground and rocking back and forth on her feet.

"Yeah, I know. Kansas is sometimes stifling. Have you thought about moving?" I offered, noticing she was very, very quiet, and now stood still.

"I mean, I don't know that I want to be here. *Here.* The pain cuts me like a knife, sometimes. I don't know… " She trailed off.

Calmly, I formulated a few thoughts into gentle words. "Could I say a prayer for you? Maybe we could look at this from a spiritual angle?"

"Please help me. I just don't know… " Silently, she looked into my eyes once again. I could see a mix of fear, uncertainty, weariness, and pain in her face. "I've got to go. The dogs will be so mad if I don't let them out. Thanks."

She stuffed the check into her bag, turned around, and walked with determination in her knee-high, black, military-style boots toward her van.

A little over two weeks from that day, I learned she was in ICU, being transferred to a psych unit. She had attempted suicide at the family home. She was discovered and taken immediately to the ER. No permanent damage was sustained, save a deep wound to the neck. The knifelike pain she had described to me had become literal. After a short stint in the psych unit, she received a discharge to stay with family.

So on that cold December night I had to see her.

As she opened the door, I glanced at her. She wore a cream-color funnel neck pullover, deep green sweat pants, and stark white athletic socks. Her eyes looked hollow, with dark circles under the lids; no twinkle, no glimmer, not even a gleam could be seen as she looked past me. She smiled pleasantly but distantly; she seemed subdued, almost vacant. As I stood in the cold outside, I prayed that my visit would warm up her heart a bit.

We spoke quietly and covered conversational topics from the weather to the holidays. We talked about egg nog, cats, Colorado, snow, mittens or gloves, and our favorite blankets. She seemed so far away, even though I sat beside her. I could touch her, but I could not seem to reach her. I could see her, but it felt as if she wasn't really there.

Finally, I spoke. "Julie, can I just send some compassion and love to you while I sit at your feet?"

"Sure," she said. "That would be nice."

I positioned myself on the hardwood floor, wedged between the couch and a coffee table. The draftiness invited me to keep a coat wrapped around me; I felt grateful for my scarf. I took a deep breath and imagined a beautiful light surrounding Julie and me, then glanced up at her. She had closed her eyes and looked a bit more relaxed. I closed my eyes, too, then softly placed my hands on her ankles to share a simple human touch, a physical connection, a kind gesture. I wanted her to feel nurtured and to know that I cared.

We sat in silence for a moment, me on the floor, her in the chair, when I heard her yell out at me, "*Let me go!*"

This startled me, and I looked up. She sat, serene-looking now, eyes closed, lips in a near smile. I wondered if I had imagined her words.

Closing my eyes again, I placed my hands on her knees and imagined more light and love surrounding her. The peaceful silence was broken once again by her loud announcement, "*Stop trying to fix me! Love me, and let me go!*"

I knew I could not have imagined this—I heard the words as clear as any. My eyes flew open to see her position unchanged save for the full smile now spread across her face.

"What did you say?" I whispered.

Her eyes still closed, she answered, "Nothing. I am just sitting here."

"Oh, sorry," I replied. I closed my eyes again and heard,

"*Don't judge me. Love me! Now!*"

I pulled my hands back as my eyes opened. No longer comfortable on the floor, I got up and returned to the seat beside her. She sat still. I could see that she had relaxed.

"Julie, I don't judge you. I just don't understand. But I do love you," I replied aloud to her silent shouts.

This time she opened her eyes and looked at me, the sadness returning, her smile slipping away. "I know you don't judge me. I am glad we finally met. I am a bit tired now."

I understood this as a cue to leave. Respecting her request, I prepared to go. She walked me to the entryway and thanked me for coming.

"I want to talk to you again soon. May I come back?" I asked as she opened the door and stepped outside with me.

"We'll talk," she called to me as I hustled to the car. "We'll talk."

Getting into my Honda CRV, breath visible and hands shaking, I started the engine, backed slowly into the street, and drove toward home. I watched as the darkness swallowed up Julie. I shuddered, but not because of the cold.

Driving home, I felt completely disoriented. The experience with Julie left me teetering on the edge, questioning what I thought I knew. If her words were true, if part of her believed that loving meant accepting and that accepting meant allowing and allowing meant letting her go, then…

Then what? Was death the answer? Did she need to go? Was something calling her?

If I were to be authentic in my acceptance and genuine in my love, I would have to choose to authentically accept and genuinely love her, no matter what.

Hours later, head still spinning, in the darkness of the midnight hour, I grabbed my coat and stepped outside. I walked and thought and thought and walked, oblivious to the weather or traffic going by, completely lost in tumbling, crumbling beliefs that were now and forever changed.

I thought I was a healer, a helper. I thought I could heal her, help her. I thought that life was always the right course, that staying was morally superior to going. But I could not hold on to those thoughts. Never again! Forever changed, Julie had released such a charge in my heart and detonated such a blast in my mind that I had to engineer a new construct of beliefs and a new structure for understanding.

In time, I arrived home. I crossed the threshold, tossed my coat aside, and grabbed my phone. Heart thumping, palms sweating, mind clear, spirit strong, I messaged her: "*I choose to love you, no matter what!*"

She did not respond.

Three weeks later, my eldest daughter hosted a party at our home, and Julie received one of the first invitations. With no RSVP received, I was uncertain as to whether or not she would be able to come.

When the party was in full swing, I decided to offer cake and refreshments to our jovial guests. Carrying a tray into the living room, I stopped short. For an instant, in what felt like an endless moment in time, I saw Julie sitting on the end of the couch, turtleneck sweater, mom jeans, and knee-high black, military-style boots, looking at me with a twinkle in her eye and a mercurial smile. She looked at me, then into me. I blinked, and she was gone.

Julie was gone.

That night, after the guests were safely home, the dishwasher loaded fully, and the counter tops cleared neatly, I got the call. Julie had found her way back home. She had committed suicide.

Hearing the news, a flood of emotions poured through me. Tremendous sadness, a deep ache, waves of guilt, and then a powerful still calm. A feeling buried inside came to the surface of my heart. Perhaps loosened by the vision I had had earlier that afternoon, or unearthed by the experience where she silently screamed, I felt an overwhelming sense of her relief. Rather than sensing a harsh ending, I had a glimpse of her rebirth. Like an unstoppable, bright, and fiery sunrise, she had become the light emerging, chasing back the darkness, heralding a new dawn.

I sank farther into this feeling, dipping my heart into a healing pool of hope. Beyond the human loss of her body, I felt an enormous, eternal gain for Julie's spirit—a free, unencumbered, unbounded soul now dancing in the light.

I experienced a glimpse of Julie, this amazing woman, this friend in life and teacher in death, awakened in joy. While I grieved her loss, I also felt something more: the death of her body was liberation for her soul. No more pain, no more hurt, no more missing home. Julie died so that she could live free. Through tears I smiled and between sobs I laughed.

Julie wasn't lost. Julie found her way home.

As Julie's sweet soul was delivered into the light, something birthed in me that evening. I determined to disarm my heart and cleanse my mind from any preconceived notions about suicide. I decided to immerse myself, a willing student and apt pupil, into the twilight class held between life and death. I dared listen to Julie's wisdom and heed her advice: Don't judge. Love.

I dedicate this book to Julie—not because of her tragic end but because she showed me a new beginning.

CHAPTER 1

End to Begin

"MOM, WHAT'S SUICIDE?" I asked from the back seat of our family's Chrysler station wagon as we traveled northbound on the "highway to Heaven," the road to our fundamental Baptist church.

I had first seen the word a few days before. During the closing credits of a rerun of the television show *M*A*S*H**, the title of the show's theme song flashed onscreen: "Suicide is Painless." Ten years old, a lover of books, a seeker of knowledge, and a student of broadcast television, I wanted only to deepen my vocabulary.

My mom, in the passenger seat in front that day, turned around and looked at me with wide-eyed surprise. Gracious, gentle, and God fearing, she believed in heaven and hell. Every Sunday, she dressed us properly and directed us firmly in church conduct and the Baptist teachings, so that our souls could stay with her into eternity.

Her devotion to the church was a blend of sincere spiritual satisfaction mixed with a desire to quell a mother's inextinguishable grief. She had lost her first child, my brother, when he was just a toddler and before he was christened at the church. Although she believed that he waited for her in Heaven, she ached for him daily and battled breaches of faith and moments of doubt because of her failure to wash his soul clean in baptismal waters. She would not make that mistake twice.

My younger siblings and I had been saved and baptized in the church. Wanting to please my parents, and seeing how happy it made my mom when I learned from my Bible, I set about making a name for myself in the congregation. Quickly, I learned the books of the Bible, memorized the Ten Commandments, knew the 23rd

Psalm by heart, and could name every piece in the Armor of God. I committed to memory over 100 verses, and won Bible Trivia Bowl at the tender age of 10. Not only could I be found in church; I was *into* church. This did my mom's heart good.

Not understanding the meaning of the term "suicide," unable to fathom the intense and sensitive nature of the topic, and incapable of realizing how Mom most likely would imply a personally terrifying meaning to my question, I recoiled at her response: as she turned in her seat and looked me in the eye, she spoke quietly but with an ardent fervor.

"That is a sin against God. Never speak of that. It is wrong."

I felt my face flush and my stomach knot. How I wished I could retract the question! Not only had I upset my mom, who only wanted my safety, but I had also dabbled with defiling myself against God. I promised myself that I would not use the word, nor further my efforts to understand its meaning for the foreseeable future. At the time, that seemed the best I could do to make amends, to make my wrong right.

Several years later, in a literature class, I stumbled on the word as I read our assigned story. Typed in bold, "suicide" was a term for which we were to write a definition. Dutifully I did so, feeling uneasy. This magnified as I read the true meaning. Although I understood, I could not fathom the concept. How? Why? What would cause a person to do that?

In 14 months' time, though, I would be thrust headlong, forever changed, into an experience with suicide.

Setting aside the whim and whimsy of elementary Sunday school, I had made my way, a fledgling teen, into the church youth group. Each and every week, like clockwork, eight to 10 of us would gather to hash it out, spill our guts, laugh and cry, fall apart, then put ourselves back together with prayer, God, and a hug or two. From issues of global consequence to topics of seeming insignificance, nothing seemed off the wall. Mixed company, different ages, banded together for a common cause: We were finding a voice to speak about our struggles, our beliefs, our understanding of God.

I felt particularly close with a female friend in the group; she and I attended the same school. Where she was a little bit country, I was a little bit rock and roll. She got the guys and I got the grades. We encouraged each other and laughed so much.

She invited me to get to know one of the boys in our group; being shy, awkward, and considering myself rather plain, I generally steered away from those of the male persuasion. But this kid was geeky cool, approachable, and seemed to me a likeable friend. Pleasantly surprised by his attitude, at ease with his down-to-earth approach to life, and comfortable with his open-hearted actions, I discovered him to be a great friend.

Over the course of a year, I took part in several overnight "lock-ins" with my church friends, rode together to contemporary Christian concerts on big conversion buses, bundled up for a few youth hay rides, and even participated in a "haunted by sin" house with my peers. During that time, a song called "Friends" was played often on the radio. The lyrics spoke to the forever nature of friendship and that the love of a friend simply would not end. We decided to make it "our" youth group song.

But one day, the music stopped, the lyrics were exposed as a lie, and the song suddenly seemed cruel and untrue. There was an end.

After a weekend outing with distant relatives, my family returned to our sleepy town on a Sunday evening. It was unusual for us to miss church, but something more unusual awaited us as we approached our driveway. With a car parked in front of the house, I could see two of my friends from youth group sitting on our front porch. Instantly, I knew that all was not well, and my stomach felt tied up in knots.

We pulled in slowly, and I could see my friends crying and motioning to me. Opening the door cautiously, I stepped onto the hot asphalt of our single-car driveway and heard a friend saying, "He's dead. He's gone. He killed himself this weekend. Steffany, he's gone."

"Why are you saying this to me," I raised my voice. "Why are you even here? He's fine. I need to study tonight. I have a test tomorrow." My face felt hot, and I wanted to go inside.

"Steffany, listen. It's over. He's gone." In the next few moments, the friend relayed to me the last few moments of his life, frequently sobbing.

No one could understand his suicide. No one was prepared. Without warning, in the wake of an argument with his brother over a hairbrush, he grabbed a gun, locked the door, and it was done.

I refused to attend the funeral; I would not acknowledge the pain and anger I felt. For so long, I had tried so hard to be so good at seeing God in everything, and finding blessings in all things. My friend's suicide shattered my innocent, naïve view of the world; he stripped me of my sunny outlook, my cheery view. Oh, how I hurt! I did not want this. I could not even cry.

The ending of his physical life marked the beginning of the end of my attachment to religion and my blind acceptance in God. My friend's suicide left so many questions and so few answers. The impact on the church congregation was so great that, after an appropriate period of mourning out of respect for the family had passed, our pastor held a Sunday night session, "Ask the Minister." Never before had something like this been offered. I asked my parents if we could attend.

The church auditorium seated about 200, and that night the space was a little less than half full. As I looked around, from the wing of pews on the right side of the pulpit, I noticed several congregants scribbling in notebooks. Most present were middle aged or younger; there was no music that night, no choir, no band. As all eyes turned to the minister, his eyes turned upward to God.

The first few questions were, though perhaps important, rather unremarkable. Then, a plucky young adult, a woman who was single, raised her hand, stood and spoke.

"Salvation is forever. Correct?" she began.

"Yes, absolutely," replied the minister. "Once saved, always saved."

"Okay, and Heaven is real… Paradise. Correct?" she continued, her cadence quickened.

"Yes, the streets are paved with gold. It is God's home," replied the minister with zest.

"Then," she paused, breathed, stood quiet for a moment. At last, her question rang out like a shot fired in the night, "Then why aren't *all* Christians killing themselves? I am tired of this place. Earth is hard. I want to go *home*." She stood, watching, waiting, as all eyes looked at her.

An intensity of feelings I had never before experienced surged through me in that moment. I could feel my emotions running through me like a current. I felt overcome with compassion for the pastor, who seemed a bit shocked; with tenderness for this young woman, who wanted to go home; with a personal angst and sense of demanding an answer; and with anger toward a supposedly loving God who would make such a hellish place for his children that his progeny would self-destruct for a chance to go home.

I felt hot, full, ready to scream. The question was not mine, but I needed an immediate answer. I dared not breathe as I waited. How could God let suicide happen? Why did God watch as my friend took his life?

The minister looked around. Suddenly I remembered my mom's words about suicide, spoken years ago. "It's a sin against God."

He spoke, seemingly hearing my thoughts. "Suicide is a sin against God. Only God can call you home. You must wait for God's time."

"So you're telling me that God calls Christians home by letting them get tortured and murdered, but he won't let you in if you've quietly excused yourself from Earth? If a Christian smokes and gets lung cancer, God calls them home by giving them cancer, but if I take pills, God won't let me come home? That is unfair." She spoke loudly, then sat down.

"Suicide is not the natural course… " began the minister.

"But murder is?" she interrupted.

"We just don't know. God is loving and merciful. And your salvation is assured. But only God can call you home," he finished and called on someone else, all too ready to move on.

Heart aching, anger seething, body reeling, mind completely numb, I, too, was ready to move on. Religion could not give the answers I needed to help either myself or others around me. In contrast to the title of the song, suicide did *not* seem painless. Suicide hurt.

Shortly after the suicide of my friend, and following the pastoral Q and A, our church was torn asunder, split in two. During the midst of the dissolution, I withdrew from religion. I didn't know how I felt about God, Heaven, or the hellish place my earth had become.

With my college years approaching, I wondered if, perhaps, the medical field would offer answers. Soon, I decided to pursue training to become a registered nurse.

Campus life proved satisfying on many levels, and one of the most important aspects of the contentment and ease I felt was the reality, the proof, the solid and testable answers that science and medicine could provide. Set values, specific norms, clearly defined parameters served as security for my head while my wounded heart stayed hidden. Living in academia, I felt confident, smug, assured. Sunday mornings were the perfect time to study and sleep in.

After successfully completing training, obtaining licensure, working a stint in acute care, and enjoying giving love and attention to my patients, I decided to apply for a job as a psychiatric nurse in an inpatient adult unit. The sadness, the pervasive hopelessness of that floor of the hospital weighed on me heavily. Daily, I dispensed enormous doses of highly potent and physically addictive pills that could just as easily harm as heal. I witnessed electroshock treatments, and spent a great deal of time listening to stories I wished I would not have to hear. So much sadness is borne in the world. Too much.

One afternoon, a quiet young man was admitted to the unit. Short in stature, he wore glasses and spoke respectfully to the staff and everyone on the unit. He seemed different. During the nursing intake assessment, I learned that he had struggled with depression and had made multiple suicide attempts. Most recently—and the reason for his admission—he had attempted to hang himself but was discovered before completing the act.

I would sit with him in the lunch area, and he would talk with me about how tired he felt. He was tired of hurting. He was tired of talking through his problems. He was tired of going to therapy, working with doctors, avoiding family, struggling to get by. He was tired of being disappointed in himself, and tired of being trapped in a dark life. He didn't like pills, he didn't like medicines, he didn't like who he was. He had tried and failed too many times. He wanted out. He spoke over and over that he was "just done" with life on Earth. He said he wanted to feel better, but to get better, he believed he needed to go back to his point of origin, to his home.

One day, during a group session, he spoke up.

"I know I was somewhere before I came here, to Earth," he said, looking around.

There was a dark-haired young man sitting next to him who had cut himself in a fit of rage and ended up in the unit. "Yeah," he said. "You're a man, so wasn't it Mars?"

Ignoring his peer's comment, he softly continued.

"I mean, I was somewhere before here. To get better, I think I need to go back there, to figure out what's what. I need to go back to the place I came from. I think that's my home."

I considered what he had said and asked him: "So do you have to die to get back there? There is no place like that on Earth?"

"Well, I think I've tried everything on Earth. I think the answer is not here. But there," he waved his arms. "That's not what anyone else in my family considers better… " He trailed off. He didn't know how to reconcile the feeling that "better" to him meant letting go, when everyone else said that "better" was going on.

I wanted to help him somehow, but I did not have answers. So instead, I just listened to him. I smiled often and listened to him talk on and on. On one occasion, I asked him, "Do you think your family would be better off if you were gone?"

He replied: "Yes, I truly do. I am a complication. The whole world would be better if I were gone."

I looked at him with compassion and spoke honestly, saying: "I will tell you something from a professional perspective. No matter what you think, your family would hurt forever if you leave. They would struggle to move on. I have never heard anyone express happiness over a suicide."

Two weeks later, he left the hospital to return to his house. A week after that, he fulfilled his desires: his final suicide attempt was successful. I learned this because his family called the unit to request I be informed. He had kept a journal while in the hospital that was found after his death. He mentioned my name, described me as kind and caring. He had written that I accepted him. His family wanted me to know.

The staff declared his treatment a failure. I, however, felt an enormous mix of emotions. My treatment of him, how I had treated him, seemed to have been a success. Still, I struggled to understand how he could not consider himself a good person. Why did he have to hurt? And where did he go? If there was a soul left of him, where was it located? Was he happy? Did he find what he was looking for? Did he discover that place he called "home?"

Remembering that religion could not offer satisfying answers, I realized this was the case with medicine, too. Despite the triumphs of the field, regardless of the wonders of the biotechnical and pharmaceutical industries, we are complex and intricate spiritual beings that transcend our physical body.

We emerge from the darkness of the womb of creation into the cradle of our mother's arms. After a journey walked, feet on the ground, we slip out of the dense body of tightly packed cells and into a vast unknown. The mystery of life, the great beyond, the nature of eternity, and the journey of souls remains secret, unmeasured, outside our control.

When considering death, my heart longed for comfort, and my soul yearned for rest. I wanted to understand, or at least to find peace with, the truth about spirit and suicide. Religion could not soothe me, medicine could not satisfy me. I wanted something more. Facing the reality of death, the hurt of suicide, and the vast chasm of uncertainty between Earth and what darkness might lie beyond, I began to feel swallowed up; a hollow sadness engulfed me. What else could I turn to? What could give me more?

Spirit!

After many tears shed, after walking through shadows and darkness, after calling out, crying hard, collapsing into a place of such confusion that I could only be still, I was birthed anew. Feebly at first, scared and lonely, I took a journey of uncovering, discovering, remembering the wisdom that resided within me. Rather than stuffing my head with facts, I emptied my mind and opened my heart to the possibility of life in a way I had not have thought possible. I had to.

I considered that we are spirit first, that we are essence shaped and molded to physical likeness, then we return, conscious, to that place where our essence formed. Time and again our essence is shaped, molded, made manifest as physical. Time and again, we return to spirit, as essence we dwell.

Daily, for moments in time, but not of time, I would sit and listen. Rather than just noticing sounds, I began listening for answers. I sought nothing; rather, I patiently waited for all things to be revealed. I listened for silence. I listened for stillness. I listened for wisdom. I listened... I would sit at the mall and listen to the quiet underneath the noise. As I talked with family and friends, strangers and acquaintances, I listened to what was not spoken. I listened to truth behind the words. For the first time in my life, I could hear! I could hear, if I chose to listen.

Quietly, softly, daily, I would listen.

Then, quite by accident, I discovered that I could hear something more. When I became truly, deeply quiet inside, still, motionless, perfectly calm, I could hear clearly voices spoken into the world from beyond. I could hear children laughing, old men telling jokes, women chatting over coffee. In my quiet listening I had discovered a broadcast band on the Heavenly radio dial.

I tested these experiences with friends, speaking out loud the messages from the voices I could hear. I practiced with willing participants. Without any prompting from the person in front of me, I would listen for the spirits around me, joining the conversation.

Rather than feeling afraid, I felt relieved, for not only were these spirits happy but the souls with whom I spoke were at peace. Deep peace that passed understanding began to percolate in me as I saw a way to understanding, a way to healing, a way to taste eternity. I could, for the first time in my life, see hope, goodness, and the spirit of God.

I left behind my job as a nurse so that I could listen to those whose spirits would speak and whose loved ones left behind would listen. An accidental medium, I blossomed into a nurse for the soul. The opportunity to assist individuals physically living and experiencing grief by speaking to the deceased brings joy to my heart and satisfaction to my soul.

One afternoon a woman came to visit with me, to hear from her loved one on the Other Side. I knew only her first name; that was enough. As she sat down across from me, I began to listen.

I heard a voice, a boy's voice and a loud one, request of me: "*Tell my mom I'm sorry. It was not her fault. Please, tell her I am happy. I am okay. I found our puppy in Heaven. And most of all, please tell her I love her.*"

I then listened to his essence, his consciousness, unmolded but clearly defined, nonphysical but very real, tell me of his life and of his transition into the vast unknown. As he shared his story, recalling the events leading up to his self-inflicted, fatal wound, I began to feel a bit dizzy; time became blurred. His last moments echoed those of my friend from church: the frustration, the fear, the fatal blow.

As if responding to me, connected by the memory, answering an unintentional call, I heard the voice of my friend from church! I could see him, smiling, as he explained in his familiar voice: "*If a suicide attempt is a call for help, suicide is the call to Heaven, 'I'm coming home. Hello! I'm coming home.'*"

The two spirits were joined by a third: I heard the quiet voice of my patient from the psych floor. He said, "*We want acceptance. We seek only love.*" I had not expected to see his spirit. I felt such love.

Those who commit suicide, in the physical life and in the space that is just beyond, want acceptance and seek only love.

And so it is for every one of us. We all want, each of us needs, acceptance and unconditional love.

As I ended the conversation with the woman before me and those spirits joining me, I realized something profound had occurred. I had experienced a moment of what I had for so long been seeking: a glimpse of life in the hereafter for souls committing suicide. The darkness slipped away as I clung to the light of a new dawn.

CHAPTER 2

Awake and Alive

"HE WON'T KNOW MY NAME. I don't think he ever heard it. But please tell him that he did hear my message. Most of all, tell him thanks for letting me go. I'm free now. Thanks!"

As I listened to the spirit of a middle-aged man share these words with me, I winced. I am aware that some in our society do not understand nor support the type of work that I do: reaching out to the right medium is alright for some, but for others, it's all wrong.

Thanks in part to the medical community's support of a healthy spirit to promote a well body, alternative healing practices are now given a rightful place in a balanced life. Despite these strides, though, psychic arts remain cloistered in stereotypes, misunderstandings, and misperceptions. Part of my heart's desire, and what I work at with such sincerity, is to give personal validation, viable evidence, and specific details from the spirits with whom I speak.

Sometimes, when I am alone, I am surprised at the wonder of it all. My religious upbringing disallowed connecting with spirits of any sort, even angels. Intuition was dismissed as silly whimsy, as a form of escape for those lacking intellect. This skewed mindset toward inner wisdom and the sixth sense was further entrenched as I strove hard to make straight A's in school. I enjoyed memorizing facts, crunching numbers, savoring details of historical data. My five senses served me well and made sense.

Then, a few years after my friend's suicide, struggling with the senselessness of his death, my intellect was dealt another tremendous blow. My mom, the sweet Christian woman who spoke wordless volumes with her quiet strength, was diagnosed with lung cancer. Never did she smoke, not a single huff nor a solitary puff. She embodied clean living. But the disease consumed her body, ravaged her insides. Worse, it eroded her faith and crumbled her hope.

The surgeons were puzzled and could not help her. The doctors were stumped and could not treat her. The researchers were baffled and could not offer options. And God? God could not help, or worse, perhaps, would not help. Several months after her diagnosis, she was dead. No more laughter, no more smiles. Only tears flowed. She was gone.

Though physically healthy, I felt dis-eased. My body ached, my soul hurt. Another senseless death, another unnecessary loss, another example of tragedy unprevented by a supposed loving God. Yet, her death rebirthed me.

As I uncovered and reclaimed my abilities to speak with those spirits who had departed, with those souls that had moved on, I felt a triumph, indeed, but this was mixed with a hint of angst. For although I chose to abstain from religion, I yearned for a connection with a divine being, a loving creator, a force for good, God. Because of my religious upbringing, my formative beliefs about intuition and spirit communications, I struggled, wondering if my abilities somehow defy God. Though no longer the little girl fearing God from the back seat of the station wagon, I still yearned for acceptance and love.

One day, opened my Bible. Admittedly I had not done this in quite some time, but I sensed that something in the pages could shed light on my situation.

I had kept my childhood Bible, the King James Version, tucked away in a cedar hope chest my mom had given me shortly before her illness struck. The random sampling of items I discovered in the box as I rifled through, searching for the Good Book, represented some of my adventures: a map of Paris, some postcards from Greece, an anatomy workbook from college, a children's book I had written in high school, and my graduation cap. The Bible rested at the bottom of the stack. As I opened it, I noticed a trifolded piece of paper tucked into the middle. I pulled back the edges and recognized my mom's handwriting. Undated, the note read:

"*Dear Steffy, I am very proud of you. You are a good daughter. Love, Mom.*"

I fought back tears and shuddered. Perhaps coincidence, maybe not. Then, I fanned through the pages of the Bible and randomly stopped. A verse seemed to leap off the page at me:

"For every good tree bears good fruit. (Matt 7:17)"

The fruits of my labor seemed good. In fact, those whom I served seemed tremendously healed, greatly relieved, and restored in faith. Perhaps my work was a good fruit.

Rather than polarizing the issue of speaking to spirits as either good or bad, defiant of God or silly fancy, I embraced this: if I believed that God had taken away those I loved through senseless death, perhaps my abilities were an extrasensory means or restoring that which had been lost: my faith. Perhaps speaking to the spirits of those who have passed was a means to span the painful gap between Heaven and Earth. Maybe I could be loved by God and be in communion with angels. I could love God and serve my brothers and sisters, physically present and those of spirit.

Remembering this brings me comfort, renews my faith, and soothes me with a deep sense of peace.

People assume, and falsely so, that when I am in working mode, as a medium, I know everything, all the nitty gritty details, about the spirits to whom I speak. I can't possibly, and I don't want to.

I learned this early on, when an adult daughter, speaking with her deceased mother, asked me, "So, ask my mom what was in that journal that she burned. We all want to know, and *you* will tell us."

I looked to the spirit of her mother, posing the question. "*That is none of my daughter's business, and it is certainly not any of yours. Butt out! Tell my daughter there was a reason I burned it!*" came the indignant spirit's reply.

Often I am asked about lost items or missing objects. One woman asked her deceased, estranged husband for the location of his hidden cash box. His spirit answered curtly, "*Oh, it's still hidden. Tell her not to worry. She won't find it. I hid it good!*"

Sometimes, a wife may ask me if her husband is having an affair, or a man may ask if his girlfriend's child is really his daughter. I don't answer these questions; although I may speak to the dead, I am not interested in looking at skeletons in the family closet.

I honor the right to privacy and respect intimate information of both the living and the souls who have moved on. I am not into sensationalism, extremism, exploitation, nor deceit. I am in this for life. I choose to speak for the deceased so that all may live free from the fear of death.

I believe this especially important in easing the pain around a death by suicide.

So when the spirit of the man refused to reveal his name, I hesitated with the message. My sense of caution rose higher still as I considered the man sitting with me. Tall, elderly, rugged to nearly hardened, he was rough, tough, made of strong stuff. His commanding presence served him well as a lieutenant for the homicide unit. I suspected that his skepticism would brush aside so vague a sentiment.

But the man's spirit kept waiting, wanting me to speak. "Listen," I spoke as I looked the policeman in the eye, "There's a man who hanged himself who has a message. He says that you did hear him. And he says thanks."

Far from dismissive, the countenance of this strong, seasoned officer shifted. His lips parted, and he asked me to repeat. Then he shared his story.

"I have never spoken this to anyone. I couldn't; I didn't want anyone to think I was nuts. Years ago, we got a call and went into a house. We found a man hanging, clearly by his own hand. The other officers started to intervene, but I looked at him. He was nearly gone. Then I heard, as clear as a bell, a voice yell out, '*Leave me! I'm done.*' I felt frozen. The man hanging there could not have spoken, but I swear I heard those words. Then I told the men to leave him. A few seconds later, he was gone.

"And now, you are telling me that I did hear something? That man was ready to go?" He asked, almost incredulous.

"I'm not telling you that. He is. I'm just reporting what I hear," I replied, sincerely.

"Thank you," he answered. "I always want to show respect, and as I heard that voice, that day, I felt that I had to let this man go. Thank you for that message. Thank you."

Another day, I heard a similar story.

"*I was ready to go,*" spoke the spirit of the young woman. I could see her image, fiery bright, big red hair with even bigger bangs. Without any warnings or indications of wanting to inflict self-harm, the 30-something single mom, momentarily alone as her child played at a neighbor's house, ended the reign of darkness in her heart and breathed into the light. "*I was so ready to go.*"

She had left behind a dear friend, a woman seeking answers, wanting to understand what happens in the afterlife. Sitting across from me, she wiped back a tear, and said, "She was ready to go?"

"*I was. Please, tell her I was,*" replied her friend. "*I had endured so much abuse, so much rejection, and so much disappointment that I could no longer stay. I wanted better. I wanted more. The only way I could see to get better was to get moving.*"

No one could have stopped me. I had made up my mind. I was ready to go."

From a spiritual perspective, the difference between a suicide attempt and the completion of the act is readiness. When the self-inflicted wound deals the fatal blow, the soul has reached an alignment with leaving the body, moving forward, walking onward and into the light. If this full readiness is activated, if this powerful, soul-level clarity is achieved, resistance from the outside will be quickly thwarted by the overwhelming strength of the soul breaking free.

Imagine stopping a tidal wave with a knee-high wall of sand. The unaffected waves will crash against the shore, washing away castles on the beach but offering new treasures from below. Consider delaying the sunset by pushing against the sky. The sun cannot stop from setting, nor can it refuse to rise.

These are forces of nature, unharnessed, untamed, unstoppable. Just as sure, the nature of a soul aligned with the full force of determination to complete a goal or to accomplish an act is nearly as impossible to contain.

Those who are left behind by suicide must understand that, when the suicide has been successful, it could not have been prevented. A powerful statement of self-liberation from a struggling soul is made: the only way out is to let go.

Before death, those who commit suicide feel an extreme polarity within: days, weeks, months, years, sometimes lifetimes of stagnation are suddenly matched and met by an intense and urgent need to make an immediate change. The contrast between the pain of reality and the possibility of freedom from the darkness is so vast, so raw, so catalyzing that the individual feels compelled, pushed, swept up into the act. Suicide is intense passion, extreme emotion, desperate desire for something more, something better, something, anything but the ongoing pain of the moments before.

By design, the soul must grow, stretching beyond its boundary of the moment just before. Trees reach, galaxies sprawl, flowers unfurl; the desire to command our surroundings and to determine our destiny is constantly on an upward curve. We want more. To settle is to stagnate. Life grows.

When the stagnation is suffocating, when settling stifles the soul, death, even by suicide, will forge a new way for expansion.

For those who commit suicide, physical existence feels like a spiritual wasteland, barren, inhospitable, dry. Upon death, the soul moves forward to frolic in fertile fields of eternal Summerland, to plunge into the healing waters of spirit to be restored and renewed, and to dance unfettered by the trappings of earthly life. On the other side of suicide is freedom. Beyond death is life anew.

"Nothing was going to stop me. I was ready to go," the young adult man's spirit spoke to me. I could see that he was a slick, charming, good-looking guy, with nice hair, straight teeth, and a dazzling smile. With me sat his estranged wife, who carried so much guilt about his passing. She wanted to understand what had gone on.

The night he committed suicide, she had planned to visit with him after her shift at work. As she turned the key to the car, the vehicle would not start. She sat. Fifteen minutes elapsed. She tried again and, at last, the engine started. She then noticed the gas tank was low on fuel. She stopped at a filling station, but the pump would not accept her credit card. Progress further delayed, she walked inside to pay. The lonely clerk wanted to chat with her, and she could not seem to escape. She then missed every light en route to the house. Nothing about getting there came easy; no aspect of it seemed to turn out right.

She explained to me, "It was like something was stopping me from getting there. By the time I arrived, he was gone. If only…" She stopped.

His spirit spoke again, this time firmly. "*I was not to be stopped. This was my time. I had to break free. I will tell you that I did not hurt; there was no suffering. The clarity and the focus seemed to take away pain and fear. I just looked up and moved on,*" he explained.

It was his time. He was ready to move on.

The passionate readiness of those who commit suicide seems to offer a shield against pain and a buffer against fear. Determination deters suffering and clarity lends courage. When I speak with those souls who have committed suicide, all of them, every one, expresses a sense of peace in the last breath and a feeling of weightlessness the instant the spirit untethers the body.

Even for those who may be momentarily revived, the connection to the body is gone. If emergency personnel or family intervene, a physical response may be elicited, but the soul has vacated the premises. No turning back. The readied soul has moved on.

Though the circumstances of each suicide vary widely, and the reasons may never make sense from the outside, those who commit suicide share one powerful similarity: a desire for something better, a wanting for something more. Each seeks a new beginning, an ending to the old. The transformation of death provides such an experience. In the eternal expanse of life beyond the body, hope resides. All who seek something better will find that and more. Those who commit suicide find rest, feel peace.

In addition to the readiness to go, each of us plans for a time to set aside the body. There is an expression, "We are born to die. No one gets out of here alive." From the time we can understand the concept of beginnings, we are also taught of endings.

Before the soul takes physical form, we chart a path, a life course. Similar to a road map, we ready a soul course before birth. Along our life's path, depending on how goes the journey, our soul can seize opportunities to speed up, slow down, cruise, or take the exit ramp.

For most souls, three exit points are charted in the life's path, one of which will take us to our eternal home by means of a physical death.

But no matter what the cause of death, be it sickness, accident, or suicide, all souls are taken to the same place: eternity, the timeless, endless sea of unconditional love.

Those who commit suicide are attempting to regain communion with the soul. When the body is set aside, the soul is renewed, and each spirit is met with grace, understanding, and an anticipated welcome. We cannot surprise fate, nor show up on heaven's doorstep unannounced, foiling our soul's plan. Every decision in life, and even the decisions about death, are prepared for, accepted, and understood by the forces of Heaven and Earth. No soul is ever lost. No soul is ever gone.

For those who commit suicide, the only accessible way out of the darkness is to step into the light. Even through death, life finds a way, just as light welcomes the new day. On the other side of suicide is an ongoing journey, a timeless dance of spirit, an expanse for the welcomed soul.

CHAPTER 3

Been There, Done With That

A FUNNY THING HAPPENED to me in the bathroom one day. My son, who was three years old at the time, requested help washing his hands. In no particular hurry, I deliberately slowed my pace, basking in his sweetness, appreciating the innocence of youth. I have found that, sometimes, the seeming insignificant moments serve as the perfect backdrop for the most profound realizations. If we choose to savor the small blessings, to steep goodness into every situation, we learn to cultivate a deeper sense of gratitude for the gift of life. A spoonful of Heaven here and a dash of miracles there can provide spiritual stamina for the journey of life.

Standing behind him, manning the faucet, I noticed he had an intricate way of swirling the bubbly, lathery soap between his fingers. With an almost rhythmic motion, he wove suds in and out, over and through his extended digits, then onto the palms. I smiled to myself. It seemed his fingers waltzed with the bubbles, a scrub-a-dub dance.

Later, as I helped him clean up for dinner, to my delight, I observed the soapy serenade of fingers and thumbs yet again, as he swirled and twirled to clean. I smiled and thought to myself, "*Creature of habit*."

After helping him dry his little hands, I quickly grabbed the soap, and without considering what I was doing, or how I did it, I began swirling soap between my fingers! My hands, like his, performed the soapy dance.

I stopped short and let the warm water flow through my fingers and across the backs of my hands. I noticed him watching me, and we smiled at one another. In that moment, I realized that his habit was a learned behavior from an unintentional teacher. Watching me wash my hands, he duplicated my motions. Without me knowingly guiding, he followed my lead. Only in seeing his behavior, in observing his actions, did I become aware of my own. His style, his behavior, his practice was a repeated pattern, a handwashing hand-me-down.

We teach the world so much by the lessons that we live.

Is it possible that, in some cases, suicide, too, is a pattern, a learned behavior that is somehow passed down?

Evidence suggests this.

Regardless of how many hours' sleep she may have experienced the night before our session, the woman sitting across from me looked beyond tired; she appeared weary. Though not a soccer mom, she was a mother who knew what it was like to be kicked around by life.

I could tell she smoked cigarettes; her facial wrinkles, especially the distinctive lines around her mouth, belied her habit. Her hair was overprocessed, with bleached-out ends and gray roots. She looked exhausted, unkempt, uncomfortable in her own skin. I suspected that she had mustered up all the strength she had to make the trip to see me; she had driven solo nearly one hundred miles. Yet the travel across the miles seemed insignificant compared to the journey that had led her to me. As we sat down, the harrowing story unfolded before me.

"His father had his chance. I knew he would check out early. But my son. Please tell me that he found his father. I want to make sure that he is okay," she pleaded with me.

Her husband, father of her son, existed on half-kept promises and wildly haphazard plans inevitably gone wrong. He had tried every get-rich-quick scheme but only got broke fast. The relationship between husband and wife was strained, intense, passionate, maddening. On one of their first dates, she recalled that he looked her straight in the eye and said, "I'm not going to live forever, you know. I don't know how. But I just know I'm going to die young."

This dark riddle proved a prophecy come true. One day, after a job offer fell through, he came home, had a few drinks, then ended it all. As she discovered his lifeless body, she felt intense anger, recalling his words, "I'm going to die young."

She struggled to find a way to cope with his loss while maintaining a good life for their son, a high school–aged youth who looked and acted much like his father. With no life insurance, no health insurance, no severance pay, she had no benefits, no savings, and no prospects on the horizon. As the money dwindled, her hope faded. As her funds depleted, her faith began to wane.

Her son remained quiet, always watching, never saying a word. Though she wanted to comfort him, she found that her emotions toward his father were so dark, she could not offer her son a sense of lightness. She could not give what she did not have: peace.

After a few months, with no end to the pain in sight, the son, longing for escape, joined his father in the ethers. He left a note saying: "*I went to find him. I have to know he's not alone.*"

The widow and childless mother found herself swallowed in unrelenting anguish. "I have to know what happened to him," she told me. "I did my best. Was there more to do? Did I do enough?" She looked to me with longing.

Softly, I said a prayer for her, then gently I began to listen.

Her son's beautiful essence, standing tall in vibrant light, spoke. "*I always went after my dad. I always went to find him. I guess we're creatures of habit. I've found him again. This time, he'll stay around,*" he said.

What I observed from his spirit was this: this young man felt unafraid of facing the uncertainty of death because he was devoted to connecting to his father. The commitment to his father's soul was made by a free-will choice, and for this young man, the commitment carried over from life to death to life again.

The grief this young man experienced after his father's suicide was, among other things, a time of intense spiritual unrest. When his father was physically present, he could tag along, toddling in his father's shadow. With his father's body gone, who could he chase? Who would anchor him? To what could he hold on? His father had become a ghost, a shadowy specter in the cobwebbed corners of his mind.

The young man's spirit continued. "*The suicide, death, is not about human shortcoming or relationship failing. Yes, my mom is human. No, things were not ideal. But my decision was mine; she did nothing wrong. Nor could she have done better, done more, or done it sooner. This was my path to walk. Mine alone.*"

His statement, "We're creatures of habit," struck me. I asked his mother, "Did he always follow his father? Even when young, did he follow his dad?"

She set her jaw, looked down, and tore at the used tissue in her hands, "Yes," she said quietly. "From the time he could walk, he would follow his dad. From out to the garage, to fixing the washing machine, to just watching TV. Everywhere my husband went my son was sure to go. Like Mary and the Little Lamb."

She then smiled, perhaps remembering her son as a child, scampering, playing, free. "It didn't bother me, their relationship. It was, in many ways, endearing. When I got mad at my husband, when I just wanted to scream, I would remember that he was a good father, and that would bring me peace," she explained.

I considered this. If her husband had, from the time of their courtship, alluded to an early demise, and her son had always followed his father's lead, could the transition from physical to spirit, from life to death to afterlife, more rightly be seen as a continuation of the father-son tradition? Could the dynamic apparent in the relationship be a perpetuation of the pattern?

The husband believed he would die young. Yet, his wife reported that he had not made previous suicide attempts, nor had he seemed particularly depressed at the time of his suicide. Considering this, I asked this woman if a vague sense of foreknowing, born of her husband's statements of an early demise, somehow softened the blow of his death?

"Yes," reported his wife. "I was angry but not surprised. He tried to warn me. He knew."

On some level, and usually in some way, those who commit suicide will often make statements such as these:

"I don't think I'll be here forever."

"I may not have much time."

"I might go young."

These statements can offer a glimpse into the soul and can provide a perspective on life that is beyond our ordinary reality. In no way do these statements imply that suicide is inevitable, unpreventable, or unavoidable. Rather, these types of sentiments indicate that the soul is somehow aware of the possibility and, therefore, in some way, prepared. On a soul level, we have no concept of surprises. Every possibility is considered, every preparation is made for every available outcome. So vast is our spirit. We grow endlessly!

This kind of soul-level pre-knowing can be demonstrated in another way. An established professional in the medical community reached out to me with a great deal of concern. Highly intellectual, at the top of her game, she took great pride in her cerebral approach to life. But her studies could not account for what seemed to be a mystical experience. She described the situation to me.

"I had an old friend from college I had not seen in some time. One night, I dreamed about her, but it was more than just a dream.

It felt so real, like I was awake. My friend was there, and we were sitting at a table, like we would have done in school.

"In the dream, she looked at me and told me: 'I'm going to be leaving soon. I've done my work here. You were a good friend. I just want you to know that I will be fine, happy, and free.' I remember that we sat together for a while longer, then she was gone. I woke up shortly after that, but could not shake that feeling."

The woman continued to explain. "About three weeks after I had the dream, I received a call from her family. My friend had committed suicide. Her family thought of me and wanted me to know."

"Why?" she asked, "Why would I have a dream like that? I did not ask for it, and I don't know if I was supposed to stop her. I don't know what to make of any of it. Why?"

Her feelings were warranted, her concern was most certainly justified. The dream implied that her friend had, in some way, already reached a readiness to leave behind the physical. Rather than a call for help, or a request for intervention, the dream seemed more of a "head's up" to a friend.

The woman and I continued to discuss the scenario, exploring the idea that the information imparted in the dream did not obligate her to have to "save" her friend.

"When I saw her in the dream, she seemed so, so happy," she reflected. "She was peaceful. The interesting thing is that, after I learned of her death, I felt that same sense of peace; I recalled the image of her sitting at the café in the dream. When I remembered that, I was able to be strong for her family. I helped them."

I suggested: "Perhaps that answers why the experience happened. You were gifted foresight so that you could be peace in the storm, so that you would know, even after her physical death, her spirit lived on, in peace."

In this case, the soul of this woman who committed suicide realized a choice would be made, then made this choice known prior to the end of her time on Earth. She allowed my client a glimpse of her soul's path, so that after her death, my client could remain steadfast, steady in the storms raging in the wake of her suicide. An honorable and sacred task, indeed.

Another unique example of this foresight into death by suicide was demonstrated to me in yet a different way. A woman living out west reached out, and we set a date to speak by phone. At the appointed time, I placed the call, greeted her warmly, but she cut me short.

"Listen," she stated very matter-of-factly. "I don't know who your typical client is, but I can tell you that I'm not typical. My husband committed suicide. We both knew it was coming. I just want to make sure he found his grandma. And I want to make sure his ceremony was right."

Pausing only to take a quick breath, she continued.

"He had been depressed, and we went to a psychologist who offered hypnotherapy. Then, after a few sessions, we found that my husband could relax enough that he was having these past-life memories. None of us expected this, but it seemed worth exploring. In all, he viewed three past lives, and each of those other lifetimes, he had killed himself. After a time we stopped with that therapy, but we both lived with a looming thought that he would die.

"He always wanted to go on his terms. You know, it was hard for me to talk with him about that; I don't know that anyone else could have. But I loved my husband; I still do. I was so in love with him that I accepted him and knew he would have to go. This world was not easy for him," her voice trailed, giving pause. I waited.

She continued: "I thought I would feel him around a bit more, you know. Like his spirit would flash lights or give me some signs.

I guess that's really what bothers me. I just want to make sure he's okay, that he hasn't forgotten me or just totally moved on. I know he was ready. I know… " Her tone muffled, sniffing, she grew silent.

My heart opened to this woman, a stranger speaking from across the miles. The strength of the love she had for her husband struck me as incredible, almost extraordinary. To know of and find peace with his seeming destiny, his chosen fate, brought new depth to the marital vow, "Til death do us part."

In our culture, from the time we are little, we're raised according to certain ideals: do well in school, behave, find a respectable job, find a suitable mate, raise a family, retire in comfort, grow old, then pass away. And we're convinced, perhaps deluded, into thinking this is how it's supposed to be.

The woman on the other end of the line had experienced nothing of the sort. She struggled to get through school, played the part of the family rebel, bounced from job to job, then picked a mate whose time would end all too soon. The contrast between ideal and reality was stark indeed.

After a few moments of reflection, I asked her: "Do you believe you could have prevented his suicide? Was there an intervention that could have been made? Could you have somehow stopped the snowball from rolling down the mountain?"

What I was asking was: If this man was repeating a pattern, could this pattern somehow have been shifted? Could there be a gentler way to transition from physical life to the journey of spirit? Although those who commit suicide are greeted with a wonderful reception and an eternal welcome in the realm of the afterlife, individuals left behind are, no matter how enlightened, regardless of how spiritually advanced, tremendously challenged to heal the gaping wound between physical presence and the bodily separation of death.

All the prayers in the world cannot make up for a simple kiss, a heartfelt hug.

Cautiously, she answered, "He asked me to love him no matter what. I told you, we were not typical. If he wanted iced tea, and if he had had it countless times in the past, if he felt comfortable with that choice, would it be loving for me to lock the refrigerator and throw away the key? I never wanted to take from him his freedom of choice. Love means letting go of all fear. I gave him my love. No matter what he gave me, I chose to give him love. He was hurting; we both were. I want to know that he is free."

I knew her words were true. Love, for her, meant letting go of the fear of losing him. Even if it meant saying goodbye through death, she would practice only love.

Quietly, I listened for the voice of his spirit. After a moment of stillness, I heard his spirit speak. "*Under the couch, next to my computer. It said, 'Thank you. Til we meet again.' I am back home, and I am free. Thank you, my wife, for loving me.*"

I relayed his words and heard her cry on the other end of the line: those were the exact messages of his suicide note. She knew he was home. She accepted that his spirit had continued on.

We pray for those struggling. We teach of the gift of life. We reach out, intervene, we prevent, we lean into support for those who hurt so much. But if, by suicide, the body is set aside and all the pain is put to rest, we remember, the soul lives on.

CHAPTER 4

Showing Up

"GOSH, I DIDN'T KNOW I WAS DEAD! I thought my plan didn't work." These words were spoken to me by a man in spirit. During his mid 40s, a hard-working, hard-partying, hard-living guy with a hard-core sense of humor, he had succumbed to feelings of deep despondency. One afternoon, with his favorite heavy metal music in the background, he inhaled a lethal dose of carbon monoxide. He fell asleep and woke up free.

His best friend, the woman sitting across from me, wanted to make sure of a few things. First, she longed to know he was okay and that, more importantly, his dry wit and droll humor remained intact. The message I relayed from him, along with other supporting details, confirmed just that.

She smiled at me, hearing his words and said: "Only he would say that. I am glad he is happy."

By his own account, the process of releasing the body proved so effortless he believed he had not died at all! The transition from the heaviness of the physical body to the light of spirit was simply waking to a new, etheric dawn.

Hollywood inundates us with grotesque images of death scenes; unnecessary violence and graphic portrayals of physical demise that serve no good. When we are subject to such visuals, we are changed, harmed, victimized by senseless, false information stylized as truth. These images are particularly hurtful when depicting suicide.

"I've seen the movies. I've seen what happens when a person hangs themselves. Please, tell me my mom wasn't gagging, choking, struggling, or afraid. Please. I can't get those images out of my head."

One bright and beautiful spring day, when the tendrils of grass greened in the yard outside my window, as the yellow finches perched on the roofline across the way, while the warm spring breeze chased out the last chills of harsh winter, I spoke with a woman frozen in hopeless fear. As we connected by phone, I could see the spirit of her mother joining us, speaking through the voice of spirit. Her mother was quaint, perhaps a bit plain, but desperate to communicate her love to her daughter. I opened my heart and listened to her, taking all the information in.

The mother, after strained relations between them, had cut off communications with her daughter a few years before her death. She had struggled with failed relationships, and was on and off alcohol for her adult life. But the silence between mother and daughter was broken one day when a stepfather called to announce that the matriarch had hung herself. No note was found.

The mother's spirit spoke. *"Please tell my daughter I now know about her children. I've seen them grow and know their dreams. I attend all the basketball games and band recitals. She doesn't see me, I know. It's hard to see a spirit! But I am here. I am so, so sorry. I needed to go. I did not hurt. I couldn't look back. I just couldn't. I had to get out. Please forgive me."*

I could hear her daughter on the other end of the line, and I could feel a wave of emotion pass through me. Her daughter began to cry; soon the cries gave way to sobbing. I knew she was releasing layers of sadness, angst, and grief spanning many years. This was a beginning.

"She wasn't hurting? She didn't regret?" she asked me.

Her mother's spirit explained. *"I couldn't regret, hurt, or look back. I could only look forward and see the brightest light. All I could see was light. I felt light, too. I felt peace."*

"But all the stuff you see. Why all those images?" her daughter questioned.

"*Those are images of a body. And yes, my body had a reaction, too. But I am not my body. I just used it for a little while. I am, my daughter is, we all are really spirit. We lug a body around, and we think that's it. But we are more, so much more! That's what I mean in saying I didn't suffer. My spirit was greater than my body. My spirit left the physical without suffering so I could be home.*"

She elaborated. "*Please tell my daughter this: When she had her children, at the beginning of the pains of labor, she felt a little scared, a little nervous. But looking back, now that she has held her daughter and felt the joy, the memory of the pain is washed away. The feeling of joy cleanses the transient pain. Death is like spiritual labor pains. We are rebirthed.*"

"I just want to know that she is happy. She is well. I can start to move on," her daughter replied. "I can start to move on."

We've explored thus far the consistent patterns and mindsets for those who commit suicide. The intensity of the release is so powerful that it creates a shield against fear; the focus is so great that it provides a buffer against pain. Each soul reports a profound experience of lightness and a feeling of love.

What next?

In a non-suicide death, four major milestones occur as we rebirth into the world of spirit. First, as we let go of the physical body, we are greeted by those non-sentient beings who support and love us. This includes family who have departed, guardian angels, pets, even spirit guides. They welcome us to our etheric retreat. The greeting is warm and unconditionally loving. All are met by a familiar face, a genuine invitation to take a place in spirit's abode.

Whether a baby who is stillborn or a homeless, hapless vagrant on the street, all are greeted with love.

After this reception comes a process known as the life review. This is a time to completely, instantly, and fully experience the effect we have had on others, to feel at depth the impact we have had on our world. Not a final judgment, nor an after-death sentencing, this is a chance to witness ourselves and relive our life in action from the outside in.

Rather than a dread or a chore, the life review is quite powerful and serves a purpose extraordinaire. This retelling of the tale, this rewind of the choices made is liberating for the soul and brings closure for the spirit. We are able to forgive others because we understand where others were coming from. We are able to fully taste the fruits of our labor. Unseen acts of kindness that create a ripple effect on Earth become a sweeping wave of celebration in the life review. We make peace with the journey just completed because we are wide open, forgiven, and free to feel and receive deep, unconditional, soulful love.

We are well received, then we reflect and review.

After the life review comes a period of rest. The soul, complete with the life just lived, having made peace with the path taken, the decisions made, having chosen to forgive and move on, will slip into a womblike chamber for deep, abiding rest and restorative slumber. More a good night's sleep, this is a period of complete restitution for the soul. The length of time spent in the sacred and still place depends on each soul's need. What is asked for is given; what is sought out is received. When this process is complete, the soul awakens, reinfused with clarity, recharged with light, and recalibrated to life as spirit. Then, the afterlife really begins!

So the soul is received, reviews, rests, and is revived as spirit. This process is consistent, powerful, and profound.

This process is identical for those who commit suicide, save for one important difference.

I clearly remember one of my first 12-hour night shifts at the hospital during my time as a practicing registered nurse. I worked telemetry at the time; we were a step-down unit from the Cardiac Critical Care Unit and, depending on the number of beds available, we would sometimes receive patients fresh out of surgery. The workload was always intense, and most nights, I worked without an aide.

One particular evening, I was assigned a post-op patient: an elderly man with chronic health complications. In the room next door, I had been given charge of another gentleman who was an alcoholic, and, being hospitalized, was unable to drink. I was told in the report to be careful, as he was experiencing what appeared to be withdrawal. Next door to him was a woman preparing for an early-morning discharge, and two more patients on cardiac monitor. My load was full.

Early in the shift, the man who had come in from surgery started exhibiting distress. We began close monitoring. He began to improve, so I resumed standard protocol. Though I wanted the chaos to calm down, it did not, for he quickly decompensated again. This dance of monitoring and stabilizing and distressing continued for several hours. We finally called and had him admitted to the critical care unit.

Meanwhile, next door, the man with the drinking habit started to act out. I checked on him, and he spoke out in a manner that was inappropriate. I remained calm, mustered some courage, and summoned compassion. He continued to chide. After a bit of time I calmed him. He remained, despite my ongoing efforts, terse, tense, exhibiting what appeared to be signs of alcohol withdrawal. He buzzed the call light most of the night.

With the demands of the shift, I could not find the time for a middle-of-the-night "lunch" break. I sustained myself, as do many shift workers, on coffee and gum.

As I clocked out, report given and patients settled, I walked slowly to my car. One thing was on my mind: sleep. I had just enough stamina for the drive home.

I arrived at my apartment, drained in every way. My roommate, a girl a few years my junior, greeted me sweetly. I gave her a half-hearted wave, walked to my room, and collapsed, still dressed, bed fully made, into a heap. I was done.

This is similar to what happens to those souls who commit suicide. So tired from the process of living, so ready to let go through dying, so completely spent, totally finished, over and done and through with the path just walked that, after being warmly received and greeted with sweet welcome, they bypass the review, spend time in profound slumber, wake up fully healed, and then walk forward into the beautiful afterlife. All souls arrive in the same haven; yet those who commit suicide frequently decline the opportunity to review and reflect. They feel more than ready to move on.

This is understandable in many ways. When I came off the grueling night shift, I collapsed into sleep. But when I woke up, I felt work stained, teeth unbrushed, mouth dry, my mind a bit numb. Yes, I had slept, but part of me wished I would have taken a few minutes to tidy up, to settle in, to change clothes and release the day. I had not.

So it is in the spirit world with those who commit suicide. In foregoing the reconciliation and release of the life review, an opportunity to feel and see just how important and impactful the soul was is lost. Afraid to look back, perhaps fearing the worst after living through sometimes hellish conditions, they receive welcome, then plunge into deep rest.

This omission may lend to challenges in future incarnations. The life review is vital for many reasons, one of which is this: we are allowed to feel and receive pure love. We soak it up, drink it in, take every fiber of light and love into the core of our being. We come to know, beyond a shadow of a doubt, without question, that not only are we loved by Spirit, but that we are worthy, that it feels right and good and true to receive. A transformation, indeed; we are fully awakened to our true nature.

In bypassing this experience, the souls who commit suicide do not allow themselves to feel. Perhaps it's the fear of having hurt those left behind. Maybe it's the fear of feeling nothing, not even love. Sometimes it's a false belief that there might be judgment passed down or karmic debt incurred. Oftentimes it's all of these. But those souls who commit suicide can't seem to bear to look. Wanting rest, needing restoration, they let go then move on.

After the rest, in the journey into the world of spirit, those souls who commit suicide come to understand past lives, soul agreements, pre-birth plans, and why the life was lived. This is mind opening, indeed. But the review opens the heart. Without the life review experience, when the soul reemerges into life, through rebirth, there can be difficulty in feeling love and in finding a sense of self-worth.

Though the review bypass has been reported to me by many souls who passed through suicide, I came to understand its profundity when I worked with a man seeking help. He seemed, for as long as he could remember, to fall into a deep depression every spring. When the world was full of new hope, he felt lost, numb, alone. Traditional counseling had not proved helpful, so he opted for a spiritual approach.

After working with him over a few sessions, I believed that a past-life regression could help in some way. As he viewed himself in another body, in a different lifetime, he became aware that, in that other life, he had committed suicide in the springtime. At the end of the session, I encouraged him, saying, "Write for that man, that aspect of you, a life review."

He did, and reported a huge improvement. But something still nagged at him. Some stuck part inside him refused to move.

We decided to explore another past lifetime, so he regressed again. Just as in the life reviewed before, he remembered a lifetime where he had committed suicide! At the end of the session, just as before, I encouraged him, saying, "Write for that man, too, a life review."

He did. Then everything in this life began to flow; every stagnant part started to move! He found a good partner and proposed marriage. He changed his business for the good. He started feeling good about feeling good. Most of all, he let himself receive. Pattern shifted, heart open, his world came to life. All was made new.

Those souls who commit suicide often disallow themselves the rich and sacred experience of a life review. We will discuss the full implications, subtle nuances, and spiritual restitution that can be brought to this as our journey progresses.

CHAPTER 5

Look Again, See Anew

AS THE SKETCHY DETAILS EMERGED, my logical mind tried to put the pieces together. Across from me sat a middle-aged professional, a first-time client, who considered himself a man of the world. When I first greeted him, he expressed that never in his wildest dreams did he think he would be seeing a medium. I smiled at him, replying: "Well, we share a common bond. Never in my wildest dreams did I think I would be a medium. Life is full of surprises!"

Upon beginning my career as a professional medium, I did not expect to deal so extensively with those spirits who have committed suicide. My desire going into my practice was to help anyone. Were I to choose a specialty, however, I felt personally inclined to assist bereaved parents. This population had a special place in my heart; I was raised as the kid sister of an "angel child."

My parents met in high school and married the week after my mom graduated. The year was 1967, the country war-torn with social, political, and global unrest. My mom had lost her father and yearned for stability; my father, wanting to shelter her, proposed marriage. Only a few weeks after the wedding ceremony, the newlyweds received unwanted news: my father had been drafted and would be sent overseas soon.

So the young bride led her life in constant worry as my father served a tour of duty in Southeast Asia. After a few months' time he had a brief visit, and my mother became pregnant with their first child.

The pregnancy went smoothly, with hardly a hiccough, and the delivery was, by my mom's account, a breeze. Her life forever changed as she held my brother, wrapped her arms and heart around his tiny body, snuggled him all day long. The hole of my father's absence was filled with the joyous presence of her beautiful and perfect son.

Life progressed quickly. My father remained overseas for well over a year. My brother's first birthday came and went, then something started to go wrong. He woke up vomiting violently, having seizures. My mom, a military wife, took him to the base physician who dismissed it as a "flu" or a "bad cold."

He continued to have episodes and my mom sought help from another doctor on the base. He ordered a scan and some tests, the best they could offer at the time, to see what might come up.

A few months later, at the military hospital, in a room cold and stark, my mom told her toddler son goodbye. He had a brain tumor, aggressive, inoperable, fatal. On that day, a large part of her died, too.

A little over a year later, I emerged, eyes blinking, cold and shivering, crying for all I was worth. Hope restored, spirit renewed, my mom loved me with all she had; she gave me everything she could.

As I grew, I began to believe I could never shine brightly enough to heal the dark sadness in her heart. Every year, at the time of my brother's birthday, she would go to her bedroom, sit on the bed, and speak only a few words. She would talk of him, of how smart he was, how he struggled up to the end. She blamed the military and cried about the doctors' care. She wanted her son to come back home to her.

I wanted that, too. Each year she seemed to sink deeper. At every anniversary she stayed in her bedroom a little longer. Nothing could ever seem to help.

My milestones and accomplishments seemed bittersweet because, whatever I had done, he never got to do, or he would have done better, or he could have done it, too. When I decided to be a nurse, well, he surely would have been a doctor. When I received a partial scholarship, he would certainly have been granted a full ride. I felt pitted against an angel child, and I struggled to find peace with a ghost.

Just before I graduated, I had an opportunity to write an essay. The topic, given to all seniors was this: What you would do if you could turn back time?

Never had I written with such power and purpose, with such strength and feeling. The answer was so clear, so pure for me. I would give my brother back to my mom. If I could turn back time, I would take the wounds and bring him back.

The essay sparked a wave of emotion in my teachers and was shared throughout the school. My mom read it, too, of course. She cried, I cried, and it seemed to help her, perhaps for the first time, to see me, to look deep within me. She told me, "Thank you. I love you, I love *you,* too"

After her death, only a few years later, I felt a very deep peace knowing that they were together. I knew, beyond a shadow of doubt that she was holding, loving, and just being with her boy. I found tremendous comfort in this. Love had found a way through.

Yet, the memories of her yearly descent into the darkness haunted me, and as I began to claim my gifts of speaking to the spirits of in the nonphysical, I wanted to help mothers of the lost.

I have to come to understand that we are all children of a divine creator; that we all come here for just cause. I know that we all have purpose, we are given a gift, we have a heart and a mind that can choose love. No child is ever lost, no blow is ever dealt that cannot be softened with the grace of spirit and the insight of our wise and wondrous soul. Those who commit suicide, the sons and daughter of parents left hurting, feel withered, desiccated, blind to the light of love.

I serve with respect, with deep reverence, and with exquisite tenderness those living with and after suicide. This I do with a humble heart and an open mind daily. I consider my work sacred time.

I smiled again at my unwitting but willing client served by the unassuming medium, He needed my help, but as he stammered around with his words, I could see the situation felt a bit awkward to him. With a sigh of exasperation, he finally came out with it.

"So, I have a friend. He killed himself in his house. Ugly situation. The thing is, I am trying to help his family sell the house. No one will buy it. They've had three contracts on it, and each one has fallen through. The agents swear the place is haunted by this guy. After hearing about how he killed himself there, potential buyers get cold feet, or cold chills, or the creeps," he continued.

Then he leaned in toward me, asking in a hushed tone, "Is he haunting the place? Do we need a priest?"

Clearly, this man had stepped outside his comfort zone to visit with me. I respected him for that. As he asked this question, my compassion for him quickened and my determination to dispel his fears steeled. I agreed to speak to the spirit of the man who committed suicide in hopes of clearing the air and selling the house.

I quieted my mind and waited in the meeting place between Heaven and Earth. This is the space we go when we dream, during a peaceful meditation, when "zoning off" or "spacing out," and as we lose ourselves in imagination. Children often visit this space, romping as dinosaurs and playing with imaginary friends. Artists, too, dip into the waters of creativity running deep and flowing wide like a river in the space. Prophets, poets, and philosophers find jewels of insight and pearls of wisdom there. If you've ever awakened from a dream that felt so real, you've been there, too.

After a few moments, I could see a young-looking man clad in cargo pants and a pocket t-shirt. He wore thin, wire-rimmed glasses and appeared lean and tall. I noticed that his face, though pleasant, looked a bit irritated. He hurriedly spoke his name and offered some validating details as to his spirit's presence, then he bluntly spoke.

"*Tell them to quit giving me a bad reputation!*" he demanded. "*Why on earth would I hang out there! I ended my body so that I could get away. Leave me out of a bad real estate market. I'm no ghost, and I'm certainly not haunting that house. Just leave me out of this. Leave me out.*"

In no uncertain terms, this man had, through his death, expressed and demonstrated that his time on Earth was done. Does this indicate that his life force had come to its conclusion, that his soul was through? I believe not.

According to the Hindu philosophy, the soul simply cannot end. The sacred text of this spiritual tradition, the *Bhagavad Gita,* states:

Never was there a time when I did not exist, nor you, nor all these kings; nor in the future shall any of us cease to be. As the embodied soul continuously passes, in the body, from childhood to youth to old age, the soul similarly passes into another body at death.

A sober person is not bewildered by such change. (2:12-13)

Reincarnation, one of the core beliefs of Hinduism that is widely accepted by its practitioners, asserts that the soul, or jiva, is pure. During the physical experience we lose sight, then struggle to regain vision of the purity of our soul. Death destroys the body but cannot mar the purity of the soul. Each soul will don new bodies and resolve old lessons until communion with perfection of jiva is attained. Hinduism does not recognize a Heaven or Hell; therefore, there is no punishment nor eternal damnation, only wisdom to be gained, change to be made, and divinity to be claimed. All souls are pure, and must be born and die and born again until this purity is fully understood.

For years, reincarnation sat in the shelf of my intellect, an interesting concept, and plausible enough. Not until I received a phone call from a woman across the country did I experience the depth of this philosophy.

Working by appointment only, I strive to maintain a modicum of separation between home life and the world of spirit. I have learned, however, that the concept of linear time is lost in the expanse of eternity, and that, in truth, we cannot separate ourselves from spirit, from soul.

One afternoon, I answered my business phone line to hear the sobbing of a woman on the other line. She asked, "Can you please help me?" These were her only words.

Never did she offer me her name, nor did I ask. She didn't follow my company policy, but neither did I. The moment she asked for help, I could hear the voice of a young man shout, "*Please talk to my mom. Please tell her I'm sorry, but that I am coming back… soon!*"

I spent a few moments being quiet, staying still. The young man's voice came again. "*Tell her it's me. But please, let her know I'm the baby. I want to come back to get a fresh start. Please tell her that I want my same name.*"

I felt balled up in emotions as I swallowed through the lump in my throat. This mind-bending information pulled me out of my comfort zone, yet the compelling urge within my heart demanded that I speak. I gave her the message, cautiously, sparingly, knowing this woman had experienced tremendous loss.

Her son had committed suicide. A bright kid, willing to please but lacking in confidence, he had fallen in with a rough crowd. Wanting to break away from the destructive peer group, seeing his family's concerns but fearful of retaliation, he opted for a redo. He wanted a fresh start.

After I had finished sharing my impressions, the woman explained: "Three months after my son died, my daughter-in-law, the wife of my son's twin, became pregnant. We found out last week they are having a boy. The family had already decided to use my son's name as the middle name for my grandson. This is incredible," she said.

Every hair on my body stood on end, and I could palpably feel something in the air. Like stepping outside on a humid day, my skin felt a moistness, a fullness in the room. Had I not relayed this message myself, had I not heard the mother's words, I might not have believed such a thing possible. Yet, I have found that "incredible" is simply a term that indicates a limited perspective. We are unlimited, eternal creators. We are judge and jury of what defines a miracle. We each perceive a personal concept of God.

Had I known her name, I could have followed up with this bereaved mother. Yet with all my heart, I am convinced that somewhere, she is smiling, snuggling up with her little one, her lost son found.

The Buddhist philosophies and teachings on both suicide and reincarnation depart significantly from those of Christianity. Spiritual practices in Buddhism offer students mindful means of releasing suffering and detaching from the pain of the physical world. Each soul must attain a state of Nirvana, or freedom from illusion and liberation from suffering before the cycle of birth and rebirth is complete. Interestingly, the Buddhist tradition teaches that emptiness is the goal and surrender of the self is the ultimate release. Because of this, suicide is not to be condemned nor condoned; rather, it is considered in the context of intention behind the act. If an individual has pure intentions to let go of pain or to heal mental anguish by relinquishing the physical body through death, suicide can be viewed as a step closer to Nirvana.

If, however, suicide is a vengeful deed, or a decision made to cause emotional pain and anguish for another, the individual will set in motion needless obstacles and unnecessary hurdles in the attainment of Nirvana. Deliberately inflicting pain on another merely perpetuates self-suffering.

Reincarnation subsequent to suicide may be influenced by the motive and affected by the reasons for the act.

I came into a deeper understanding of this when, one crisp, midwinter afternoon, I met with a mother whose 19-year-old son battled his own "inner demons." She shared with me that he had always been "different," and seemed, "hard to reach." She feared for him, and asked me, "When do you see him getting better?"

To be certain, I do not cast fates or predict outcomes. I don't believe that we are enslaved to an inevitable destiny. In any moment, every moment, for all of time, I know from the depths of my soul that each of us wields the most amazing and immense power of all: free will. We can, with a single thought, in an instant, literally change our world.

I believe that at the heart of every decision—no matter how it looks on the outside or how the circumstances line up in the end— is a desire to feel better. Regardless of how it all plays out, we all yearn to feel better, to experience something more: more peace, more strength, more love. We want to feel good, to have a sense of ease. Even if we have to die to find it, we all want a place where we fit right in, a space that feels like home.

Suicide is not the easy way out, nor is it the "chicken exit." It is a powerful statement on behalf of the innate, overwhelming desire for something better. Suicide is an undeniable request for abiding peace that is instantly granted. The last breath is a first step in receiving so much more than before.

Wanting to honor the question posed and empower this bright woman in supporting her son in a way that kept her own spirit strong, I paused for a prayer. I imagined looking at an emotional "weather map," to see when the storms in his heart would subside and blue skies would prevail. I could get a sense of this and shared with her, "I see such light in him and around him. I just see beauty and peace for him in the fall. He will know tremendous peace!"

We talked a bit more, as I helped her understand how she could care for herself even in the midst of seeing others struggle. We discussed how she could change guilt-based thoughts around loving herself, despite the circumstances in her family. I encouraged her to value her own insight, to spend quiet moments in contemplation, and to treat herself with patience and love. She seemed deeply encouraged with the information and genuinely inspired to make a fresh start.

And she did. Then one day, in the fall, she found her son in his vehicle. He had committed suicide.

She reached out to me, reporting: "The first thing I thought of was your words… that you saw light and peace for him. I know he is free now. I know he is done suffering. And I know how blessed I feel, because I have been learning to care for myself, too. I just keep remembering: He is in light."

In the months that followed, I spoke with the spirit of this young man, who was, most certainly, peaceful and light filled. He extended deep gratitude to his family and relayed a profound message. "*Tell my mom I will come back to Earth someday, when the time is right. Not because I have to, but because I want to. I see the light here in heaven, but I want to see light there, on Earth, too. I send love!*"

On the other side of suicide is light. In the light, we walk free!

CHAPTER 6

From Darkness Here to Light There

HER EXPRESSION SEEMED PART GLARE, part scowl, part fear. I welcomed her into my office, then, looking at her I felt butterflies in my stomach. I knew she felt anxious, and empathizing with her, suddenly I experienced a twinge of nervousness, too. I spoke, seeking to put her at ease. "Did you have any trouble finding the place?" I asked.

Disregarding the question, she stated bluntly: "There are two reasons I came to see you. First, you go to church with a friend of mine. I trust her, and I know she is a good person. She told me you are honest. Second, I heard you pray before you work with people. I assume you pray to God. Is this true? Do you pray?"

I am accustomed to fielding questions about my chosen profession. Over the years, I've received questions such as:

"What's it like, to do what you do?"

"Why did you leave your nursing job?"

"Can you shut this stuff off?"

"Is it like in the movies?"

"Do you ever talk about bad things?"

Each question receives an honest, dignified reply. I recognize there are a lot of preconceived notions out there about mediums, seers, or psychics. Understanding this, I see myself as part medium, part mythbuster, part mystic, and always clear and open with my work. These two statements, and her question to follow, struck me as unusual. This, I had not been asked.

After several years' hiatus from church, and following the death of my mom, I found that the social aspects of congregating with others and communing with like-minded individuals in a religious setting offered a sense of community connection for me. So, with my husband in tow, I decided to visit a local, nondenominational place of worship. The minister spoke enthusiastically, the musicians played amazingly, and the members welcomed us warmly. I had found, on my own terms, a church home. Not out of obligation, but by choice, I attended.

Before any and all spirit connections, I do spend time in contemplation and prayer. Carving out a quiet space prior to working with the public allows me to deeply surrender into the heart of my purpose: to lovingly provide a voice to those who have moved on. I truly enjoy saying my prayers.

I looked at this woman, who had begun biting her lower lip. I knew there was a reason for these questions. I replied, "Yes, I do pray. And yes, I do attend church. What is your real concern?"

Something in my tone must have relaxed her, because her guard dropped. She looked down and spoke softly.

"My sister killed herself almost a year ago. I was so sad and desperate that I went to see a lady who said she could contact the dead. She told me… " As her voice trailed off, my heart sank. I knew my client, in her vulnerable state, had been wounded by the false claims.

"She told me my sister was in a dark place. That she was crying and alone. I can't stand to think of that. I know she killed herself, but does she have to suffer forever? Wasn't the pain of Earth enough? She said that if I followed some protocol, I could give my sister's soul a chance to see the light. I want my sister to be okay," she sobbed.

I wanted to put my arms around her for comfort; sometimes, a simple touch speaks more than words. I handed her a tissue and said, "I would like a chance to speak to your sister. I have a feeling she is happy, indeed."

Over the next hour, I listened intently to the voice of a beautiful young woman telling a story of brokenness and redemption, heartache and healing. As a teen, she fell prey to bullies and turned to drugs to find escape. At 19, she became pregnant, then terminated it through surgical abortion. She was bright and beautiful but couldn't seem to find her feet. The soul tipping point came when her boyfriend of only a few months stepped outside of their relationship. She scribbled a note and took too many pills.

Then life began anew! Her spirit described to me, in great detail, a creek with a bend, river birch trees, weeping willows, and a cocker spaniel dog. Joining her was the spirit of a kind older lady, her grandmother, and the soul of the baby she had lost. I could see her hair tucked behind her ear, two piercings in her left ear, and she told me she walked with God. The sun shone, the waters of the creek sparkled… everything, everything felt like home.

"*The moment I left my body was my first moment of peace,*" she explained. "*Let me describe it like this: My body, and my life on Earth felt like cold, soggy, wet, heavy clothes. As soon as I swallowed those pills, I felt warm, then it was as if I had taken off those cold clothes and had slipped into a fluffy cotton robe. Someone wrapped love around me; I think it was an angel. Then I saw Grandma, and the spirit of my little girl who was not born. It was quiet for a while, but I felt calm. It was just warm. This was the land of spirit.*"

"*After a time, I felt energized enough to move around. That's when I remembered the creek. No sooner did the image come to me than the place appeared before me. I am here now. No darkness, just light.*"

She concluded. "*I wasn't scolded. I didn't have to hash over all the hard times of my life. Since I arrived here, I have felt pure acceptance, palpable support, and love all around me.*"

Everything she described to me, from the details of her grandmother to the trees and the creek, was validated by her sister. The bend, the terrain, the dog were woven into the tapestry of the sisters' childhood spent together. Overwhelmed with the beautiful memories and the undeniable details, my client looked at me. "Heaven was on Earth the whole time! When we were little, we played there and never even knew it. Oh, thank you. I know she is home!" she cried, shedding happy tears this time.

As this young woman set aside her heavy physical form, she stepped into freedom, light, and a space to find and feel love. One detail that struck me about her account of her first moments of expansion was that she did not experience a "life review."

The old expression "My whole life flashed before me" captures the essence of a life review. Nearly every religion and spiritual tradition on our planet, dating back to the ancient Egyptians, describes, upon death, a chance to review the human life, to understand the personal and global impact we have had on the world.

The classic holiday movie *It's a Wonderful Life* marvelously plays out the concept of a life review. Although the hero, George Bailey, does not commit suicide, he is on the edge, literally. Without taking the leap, he is allowed an angel's eye view of the life he has been given and what would have happened without his physical presence on Earth. This corresponds with the belief in a live review found in all cultures. In eternity, once we are no longer subject to linear time or left-brained thinking, most souls will recognize, review, then renew.

As discussed earlier, we move into the spirit realm, and we are met by those we recognize who have gone before us. Even young children, infants, and pets are greeted by friendly faces. The recognition is not so much about the physical; after all, this is a place where a body cannot go; it is about a soul connection.

To understand this to some degree, consider: upon meeting someone for the first time, you feel an unexplained comfort or instant liking, a familiarity, not based on looks, but strictly on a feeling. This echoes the concept of the deep, soul recognition experienced once in the nonphysical plane. This soul-to-soul salutation offers a bond that provides deep comfort in the etheric realm and profound peace in the afterlife.

After a soul is recognized and received, the life review takes place. The generally understood and accepted wisdom is that those we love who greet and receive us offer solidarity and support through the review. Far from a sentencing or passing down of a final judgment, the life review is more accurately described as a purging, clearing, and release of the life lived. This review clears the way for a time to renew.

Yet, as with the soul of the young woman with whom I spoke, often, those who commit suicide are spared the life review. An overwhelming compassion and gentleness greets them as they awaken to new life. Perhaps the benefit in looking back to such painful experiences serves no higher good. The cost of dwelling on the heartaches of the past is just too great. When an individual commits suicide, the soul moves onward and upward, face forward, looking only to the light of a new dawn. Earthly blinders on, the focus becomes receiving love, recognizing the soul's perfect place within the whole, and restoring spiritual vision.

After being graciously received and lovingly recognized, clearing the past with a life review, the soul is then allowed a time to renew. This phase of initiation in the world of spirit provides profound stillness and timeless rest. This is the moment when every tear is wiped, every wound is mended, and all things are made new. Endless summer, eternal light, the renewal is individual specific bliss. All are invited to renew. All are warmly received.

I have found, in over three thousand case studies, that the nonphysical place to which our soul travels is unique for each of us. Heaven, perfect though it may be, is not one size fits all; it is not one specific place. The world of spirit is as diverse as our own Earth, and more so. From glorious, vibrant forests, to living, crystal waters to space-age technical cool, each soul chooses then savors the perfect place for rest. The "keys to the kingdom" allow for unlimited creativity and endless bliss accessible to all souls on the other side. The complexity, simplicity, and diversity of the etheric realm reflects the vision of perfection nestled in each of us. Heaven is the space where the soul expresses in true living color. Our experience in the Spirit World is inspired, ignited, and made manifest by spirit within .

And so everyone, regardless of the cause of death, is recognized in the light and renewed with rest. All soul receive boundless love. All.

One other notable detail stood out for me in this session. My client, the bereaved sister, remarked, "Heaven was on Earth the whole time. We played there and never knew it." This struck a chord in my heart.

Part of the pain from loss through suicide, or any separation through death, is that our loved ones feel so, so far away. Heaven seems somewhere on the outer edges of the cosmos, way, way, way up there in the sky. In effect, Heaven is unreachable from Earth. When the ones we love the most go there, we fear they, too, have become unreachable.

Because of my professional experiences, I have discovered that the nonphysical dwelling place for souls, the location of the afterlife, Heaven as it were, is simply a change in our awareness of the aspects of life we could not see from the ground level, Earth. Our spirit is not the opposite of us, but rather a different expression of who we really are. This is why I use the term "The Other Side." Heaven and Earth are one.

Right now, find a penny. Hold it for a moment. Feel the etching and the markings. Look at is from every angle—heads, tails, turned on its side. Sometimes you can see only heads, sometimes only tails. If the penny is tilted, more of the head might be seen, but it becomes obvious that the other side is there. A penny appears different, depending on how you look. Heads and tails are not opposites, per se; just two aspects of the same coin. You can't separate the head from the tail; both sides merge as one.

So, too, is the connection with our physical life and our spiritual journey. Because of this merging, we dream, we imagine, we meditate, we create "on Earth, as it is in Heaven." This side and the other side coalesce into life, and in this blending, in the space where both come together, awaits the healing and transformation after suicide.

So Heaven is here, reachable, visible, palpable; growing in the rich soil, playing at the water's edge, streaming through the cracks! As my client suggested, do we play there and never know it?

I believe the answer is a resounding yes.

"*Let me show you something*," the spirit of the teenaged boy said, as he invited me to step through a clearing in the woods as I beheld him in my heart. I allowed myself to see what he wished to show me, knowing that I would describe this to his mother, my client, a woman younger than myself, sitting before me.

I could see a beautiful lake at sunset, rippling waters playfully waved by a gentle breeze, drenched in honeyed pink colors. Tall oak trees and lush evergreens encircled the lake, and I noticed a wooden walkway leading to a small, simple dock.

As I drank in the feast of color, rich and vibrant, I noticed the spirit of the young man sitting with his back against a large tree, legs outstretched. He wiggled his feet for me; I noticed his flashy shoes. He smiled broadly and said, "*Tell my mom you like my shoes*."

As I detailed the scene for her, she gasped. "That is *his* place. We found his body there; he had killed himself around sunset. He was wearing his new soccer shoes. Are you telling me that's Heaven?" she asked.

His spirit beamed. "*Please tell my mom it is. I didn't stop when*

I died. That's what I want her to hear the most. There was no darkness. There wasn't even so much as a pause! I took a breath, then voila! Here I am. I am always here. I've been here all along.

"*When I ended my life, I wasn't whisked away,*" he stated. "*I was awakened to the true beauty that is always here. When we get stuck in pain, when we are trapped in fear, we are blind. But when my body died, my vision was restored. Really, Heaven is here, waiting. I'm awake to see it now. No more fear!*"

Without even as much as a pause between physical death and afterlife, his spirit's vision was restored. He could see beauty anew.

On another occasion, I spoke with a woman whose father had committed suicide when she was in her early 20s. As I opened my heart to his spirit, I listened for his voice to confirm details, names, and specific signs. After receiving supporting information to validate his spirit's presence, I noticed his spirit motioning to me. He directed me to look at a shed. In the background, I could hear hammering and, after a time, a handsaw grinding. I could see his spirit opening the door to the shed; inside, working at a carpentry project, was Christ!

The spirit of the man spoke. "*Tell my daughter that I decided to learn from the best! This is Heaven,*" he chuckled.

I reported this to her. Her father was happy, indeed! No darkness, nor shadow—not even a cloud in the wild blue sky. His body's ending was a new beginning. He was welcomed by a carpenter. He was greeted with love.

On the other suicide, there is a new day where the sun shines for all.

CHAPTER 7

Why This?

WITH BITTERNESS IN HER TONE, words spoken through clenched jaw, she replied to me: "Oh, that's just rich! Nothing has changed, has it? I had to pick up the pieces for him while he was here, always cleaning up his mess. Now, he kills himself, lands in Paradise, and I'm the one who is left behind, taking blame. Forget it, I don't want to hear any more. What am I supposed to do?"

The woman sitting with me found herself widowed at a young age. While most of her married friends planned baby showers, she arranged her husband's funeral. Childless, broke, dwelling in a ramshackle home, she struggled to pick up the pieces of her shattered life. Her husband, a man filled with grandiose dreams and impulsive acts, ended his life after his "best idea ever" went bust. I suspected that if her husband had been to a psychiatrist, he would have been diagnosed manic, bipolar, or borderline. But without a professional to guide him, he relied on his "luck." Until it ran out.

Yet, upon his death, he had been met with the same acceptance, love, and tenderness that all souls receive on the endless journey through time. Departed friends and family greeted him, healing bliss restored him, and a sense of freedom expanded him as he took his last breath. This proved consistent with the reception all souls receive upon their departure from the physical and arrival in the space beyond time.

Although his widow received a moderate amount of comfort from the confirmation of his ongoing life force and the continuation of his soul, she had certainly not been met with acceptance, love, and tenderness here on Earth. Rather, his family scorned her, her friends seemed absent, and no one reached out to her at work. She felt abandoned by her spouse and rejected by kin. Far from Heaven on Earth, she languished in guilt and shame.

Similarly, I worked with a group of sisters whose mother had committed suicide when each was in her teens. The matriarch's soul found peace. Her children, motherless and uprooted, found years of uncertainly, endless questions without a single answer, and lives plagued with guilt and fear.

On another occasion, I counseled a woman whose best friend had committed suicide to exact revenge on her lover. Her overwhelming anger toward her deceased friend, mixed with her own struggle to maintain faith, had begun consuming her. She questioned, "Why this?"

The range of emotions experienced by those left behind in the wake of suicide varies wildly. From anger to shame to guilt to blame, each individual moves through grief in a different way. The intensity of feelings may ebb and flow from day to day; healing unfolds in a nonlinear way. But the grief process for those left behind by suicide poses two additional challenges: uncertainty as to what is next for the "lost soul" and lack of acceptance for just cause.

With the social stigma against suicide, religious admonition with regard to the act, and cultural insensitivity toward those left behind, survivors of suicide frequently become emotionally frozen in fear. The uncertainty as to the whereabouts of the soul who has committed suicide can lead to chronic anxiety and mistrust in relationships. Additionally, the pervasive "20/20 hindsight" mentality of our society often holds accountable those left behind for not "seeing the signs" or "offering to help." One client shared with me her belief that she "should have known" her son would commit suicide. Loss is difficult enough to overcome, but loss compounded with a misplaced sense of responsibility for the outcome can seem like an obstacle that is impossible to surmount.

Indeed, any loss through death deals a tremendous blow. When I was 21, as I have mentioned earlier, I lost my too-young-to-die mom. After dealing with a particularly nasty and lingering cough, she decided to visit the family doctor. A chest x-ray revealed several tumors; pathology reports yielded the diagnosis of a rare lung cancer. Months later, body ravished, her soul moved on.

Two aspects of her death worked to my advantage in catalyzing the healing process. One, I had been prepared prior to her departure. Although I could never bring myself to say the word, "goodbye," she and I spent silent moments in understanding between us. I would sit next to her bed and appreciate the songs of the birds, the simplicity of the sunset. Some days, I would study and she would rest; we knew the time was precious, the moments few. Even as we removed her from life support, I left it at, "See you soon."

Though I prepared myself to the extent that I could, the anticipatory grief could not shield me from the actual experience of missing her physical presence. To fill in the gap between Heaven and Earth, steady and sure, awaited faith. Her decision to practice her religion and to follow the protocol for salvation provided a spiritual safety net for me in the wake of her passing. Everyone in our neighborhood, the church, the community affirmed this. "She is most certainly in Heaven! How happy she must be."

The statement eased the sting of the loss and blunted the pain of separation. Knowing she lived in Heaven, I found just enough comfort to carry on.

Contrast this with the loss of my friend from church, the young man my mom knew. Upon his death, no one could affirm his destination, nor confirm his whereabouts. The would-be safety net of faith had been cut by blades of uncertainty, shredded by doubt and fear. While the physical separation felt painful, the emotional upheaval felt insufferable in the months after his loss.

Left behind, the survivors of suicide feel those souls who leave are gone.

Although nothing can bring back a body that has perished, and though not all are open to explore or able to consider the spiritual connections that exist beyond the physical, those left in the wake of suicide can restore hope and renew a sense of rightness with the world. Suicide may be an ending, but it does not have to be a ceasing of life. Three steps provide measureable comfort and healing gain.

First, those left behind must come to a place of acceptance. To be clear, acceptance does not indicate nor imply any judgment at all; in fact, it is the absence of judging the rightness or wrongness of suicide that allows for healing to begin. Acceptance is a choice, made from conscious determination, to withdraw pain and suffering from the emotional intensity of death. Acceptance is the simple statement, "I can accept that suicide was the choice made, the path taken."

Affirming this truth, aligning with the reality of these words, offers freedom for all, for not only does it liberate the individual who committed suicide from a disempowered, victim state but it also releases those left behind from any burden of responsibility. Accepting that suicide was the choice does not justify the decision, does not find fault with the outcome, nor does it attempt to change what is. The choice to accept suicide as the decision simply calls forth strength in the moment and a willingness to be made aware of new and more positive perspectives.

I worked with a woman whose daughter had committed suicide. The bereaved mother struggled with intense anger because she truly believed that her daughter shouldn't have made that decision, that her daughter had made the wrong choice, that her daughter had done irreparable damage to the family, that her daughter was in the wrong. Trapped in this hellish prison of rage, she could find no joy in her life.

We spoke at length about her spiritual beliefs, and, in time, I asked the mother: "Do you think that if she had felt other options were possible she would have made a different choice? Do you think that she could have made a different choice? Can you accept her, and her choice, and love her all the same?"

She thought for some time, then replied, "Okay, but she didn't consider all the options! She just took the easy way out."

"Can you accept that she considered the options that were considerations for her, and from there, made a choice?" I asked.

She considered, then replied: "Oh, so perhaps she did consider this the best path for her. She couldn't consider other options. She didn't consider those left behind. But there was some type of consideration?"

"Is that possible, do you suppose?" I asked.

"Yes, of course. I am sure that's possible. Yes, that would make sense," she said. She stared at the space just above my head, lost in thought, considering.

"So acceptance does not mean I support her decision, it does not mean that I like her decision. It means that I realize that it was what happened," she said.

"Yes," I explained. "Acceptance does not moralize the decision. Nor does it excuse your daughter. Accepting her physical absence allows you to move past the emotional battle that is raging within you. When you accept that she made a decision, you can begin to move beyond the pain. Because beyond the pain is presence, and only in the present can you access peace. Peace cannot be borrowed from an uncertain future nor can it be taken from a romanticized past. Only in accepting that she is not here, at least not her body, can you hope to find a new outlook on life."

Acceptance is an amazingly powerful claim to our true, creative, spiritual power. The instant we face our circumstances is the very moment we claim our power to change our outlook, shift our perspective, and create circumstances anew. Efforts at renegotiating reality are not only fruitless but anxiety provoking, and, in time, may induce learned helplessness and depression.

Although death is not the most engaging and uplifting topic of conversation, releasing the physical body is a natural, inevitable experience that each and every human faces, ready or not. Sunrise, sunset, birth, death, the changing of cycles, the shifting of the tides, moving from the darkness of the womb, through the light of day, then back, through death, to the void again, our body grows, breathes, ends. Accepting death, then, is accepting life.

One afternoon, I met with an established client. A woman in her mid-40s, she had survived a traumatic ending to her marriage: her husband, in a rage of unfounded jealousy, killed himself as she looked on. Unable to save him, she felt a part of her died that day, too.

In our first session together, I helped her understand that her husband had found his way to the light, that he was free and forgiven. She accepted this with grace.

She accepted that he was gone. In fact, she could not deny this in any way. She watched this man die, violently, by his own hand. Not for an instant did she struggle to accept his physical demise. Her journey had taken her past the first step to healing: acceptance.

The conflict for her, then, lay in the disparity between how she believed she should feel and how she did feel. She could not seem to make herself feel good every day. A year had passed, and still, the path to peace with his transition felt rocky, bumpy, choppy, shaky. The good days were okay, the hard days were devastating.

Accepting the reality of a death through suicide is a choice to open the mind to new ways of thinking. This is a necessary step, but it is not the only one. We are deeply emotional, highly sentimental, profoundly feeling creatures, held to one another through ties that bind our hearts. Knowing that death is real and accepting it as part of life is empowering. Feeling at peace with a loss through suicide requires acknowledging the intense and wide range of emotions accompanying the loss.

The woman who accepted her husband's suicide felt a wide range of emotions, then experienced guilt over such intensely varied feelings. She reprimanded herself: If he were in a happy place, if his soul had found peace, she should let that be enough. His happiness should ensure her ease. She believed that if she were just strong enough, if she were good enough, she would be over his death, feel well and good, and all would be done.

Acknowledging our emotions is a bold statement of self-care and a proclamation of self-love. When we are willing to recognize how we feel, when we can allow the rivers of tears to flow, the streams of emotions to course, the deluge of guilt, sadness, struggle, and separation to flood out, undammed, we can wash away the pain and begin to live renewed. Rather than running from our feelings, judging our emotions, we must acknowledge how and what we feel. Then we heal.

In the first moments of our second session, she turned her focus on him. "Will you talk to him for a moment? I want to make sure he's still okay." She could not make eye contact with me as she put in the request.

Gently, I redirected her. "I would like to talk to *you* for a moment. I want to make sure you're okay. Whatever you feel, I accept you. Let's talk."

And talk she did! During the hour together, she spoke of her anger toward him for leaving her the way he did. She acknowledged a great deal of resentment that he was in a happy place and she was left "holding the bag." She felt hatred toward him, because his suicide made her look like a bad wife in the eyes of his family. She was disgusted with him for insulting her in his death and horrified with him for ending himself in such a mess. She felt scared that she couldn't make it on her own, terrified that no man would ever love her, knowing her deceased husband had killed himself. She felt guilty for being angry. And at the bottom of all this, she felt that somehow, even though she was innocent, his death was her fault.

These emotions tore through her like a hurricane, battering her soul and pounding down her heart. Every day, she battled feelings that would not go, futilely denying the darkness looming. She was angry with herself and furious with him, believing that he did not have to die.

After emptying her heart, clearing her head, wiping her eyes, she looked up at me like an innocent child lost and afraid. "I'm a bad person, aren't I?" she said.

"No, you are an amazing person. Thank you for acknowledging your feelings. Thank you for letting yourself cry." I spoke from my heart.

She smiled and said, "Thank you."

By acknowledging her feelings, she freed herself from the burden of silent suffering and needless blame. She accepted death as part of life, acknowledged her deepest feelings, then readily sought the next step for healing: accept, acknowledge, act.

Accepting the reality of physical death and acknowledging the associated feelings are inward-bound journeys. Freeing the mind and clearing the heart are conscious decisions made from within. In order the meld together the mind, spirit, and body, action must be undertaken, plans made, and choices activated that bring our environment in harmony with our healed heart and mind. We think, feel, then act.

Sometimes we need a hand to hold, a cheek to kiss, a shoulder to cry on, a waist around which we can wrap our arms. Sometimes we need to see a smile, hear a laugh, feel the warmth of a touch. Suicide steals away the body and leaves in its place a cold void.

In the moments of pain from physical absence, we must act with inspired presence. We can enliven the memory of those past by going outside, letting sunbeams wrap us. We can let the breeze gently kiss the cheeks, rest shoulders against the soft earth, cry out loud. We can smile at a stranger, listen to children laughing, stroke the soft fur of a small kitten. We act gently, lovingly, and consistently to fill the void with spirit, ease, and love. We act.

Journaling, walking, looking at old photos, setting goals, community education, fund-raising, listening to music, cooking, volunteering, resting, and creating are some ways to foster a renewal of hope and a restoration of life.

I worked with a grandmother whose grandson had committed suicide. In his young 20s he gave up hope, succumbed to depression. After his death, she found her soul stagnating and looked for something to soothe her spirit, to ease her pain.

After synchronizing my heart to the living presence of her grandson, I became inspired for her: a mailbox!

During his elementary years, for Valentine's Day, the grandmother would help her grandson create a box for Cupid Day cards. She, of course, would be the first to put a note of affection into his handcrafted container. The tradition had been forgotten after a time, but would soon be resurrected for the good of all.

Immediately after we met, the grandmother joyously designed a mailbox for her spirit grandson. She reported to me that most days she put a note into the box. Then, one day, something happened.

"I opened his box today. It sits inside, on my kitchen table. Well, when I went to deliver his note, I found a white feather inside! I suppose it dropped from one of his wings," she said.

The validation of his presence, amazing! The inspired action created profound healing.

When we accept, acknowledge, act, we find that on the Other Side of suicide is hope. Beyond death is life.

CHAPTER 8

Faultless

TOSSING ASIDE COMMON COURTESY, I rushed past my friends from church, pushed open the front door, slammed it dramatically behind me, then bolted to my bedroom. As I neared the door, my pace slowed, I took a breath, and said to myself: "*You are fine. You have homework. This is ridiculous. Pull yourself together.*"

I calmly gathered my papers and opened my geometry book. With Monday just around the corner, I needed to get to work.

I fanned to the back of the textbook for the assigned lesson. Geometry came relatively easy for me, and although it wasn't my favorite subject, it was painless enough. A slow smile spread across my face, as I discovered the first problem was a proof.

Proof. I repeated the word to myself a few times. Proof. A wonderful, touch-it, feel-it, hold-it kind of quality. Proof, something demonstrable, repeatable over time. Proof.

I tumbled it around in my mind for a few moments, losing time on my homework. I couldn't help but consider something I had not: "*What if they're lying to me? What if this is a trick, a trap, a joke? I didn't get any proof. I think this could just be a misunderstanding or a miscommunication.*"

I rather liked this thought and decided that my friend, the one who had taken his life, was in truth, alive and well. The girls were probably being mean to me for some reason. God would not allow such a tragedy to occur for a bright member of our group.

That satisfied me for a moment, long enough that I could complete homework. Preparing for bed, I gathered my pajamas and slowly paced to the narrow bathroom. I knew the warmth of the water would feel so good.

I closed my eyes and let the heat penetrate my muscles. Sitting in the car for the hours' long journey had left me a bit sore. Rubbing my shoulder, I stretched my neck as I dropped my head to one side. Water trickled into my ear.

Proof. The word shot through my heart, and my stomach knotted. As I straightened my neck and dropped my shoulders, I felt a huge lump well up in my throat. My mouth began to fill with saliva, and I thought I would be sick. I heaved, dropped to my knees, and, as the water continued running down my body, I began to sob. I could not fight back the searing tears. I grabbed my knees and hung my head. I didn't need proof. I knew he was dead.

Time lapsed again as I sat numb. Only a gentle knock at the door brought me back. My mom wanted to make sure I was alright. "You've been in there quite a while, sweetie," she said. "You're going to shrivel up, you know. Your brother needs his turn."

"Okay, Mom." I turned off the water—I had not even washed. "I'm coming. Thanks! Give me a few minutes, and I'll be out."

Grabbing a well-worn dark brown towel from the rack, I dried myself partially and dressed absentmindedly. I clenched my jaw. I would get through this. And I would feel nothing. I coached myself, saying, "*No time for that now.*"

I did not attend his services. Nor did I sign any sympathy cards. The youth group gathered for a prayer vigil. I did not attend. God had proved that He did not listen, and I was convinced that love, no matter how strong, was not the answer. Clearly, obviously, I had proof of this: Love was not enough.

Because if it were, my friend would be living, and my world would still feel whole.

After a few weeks' time, when some of the numbness had worn

off, a new, more terrifying thought started plaguing my mind and stalking my heart: perhaps the love of God was more than enough, but I was not. Maybe if I had been a better friend, perhaps if I would have stayed home that weekend, if only I had really spent more time with him. No longer able to find fault with God, I believed that I had only myself to blame. This thought nearly broke my heart, and I struggled for some time with tremendous guilt.

The desire to have someone to blame, to have a just cause, to find a direct reason for a death, seems to be a normal human quality. In our need to control, to ensure our dominion, to package everything in a neat tidy box, we often struggle to come to terms with the basic, raw truth: there are some things in our lives that may never, ever make sense.

And with suicide, when there seems no justifiable reasons for a self-imposed death sentence, when there is no substantial "proof" of what lies beyond for those souls, the gulf between the known and the uncertain, between life and death, is breached precariously by the most risky of emotions: guilt.

The intensity of this common reaction to suicide was poignantly demonstrated to me one afternoon as I worked with a woman in her 50s. She was so anxious to see me that she had actually arrived one week and one hour early for her scheduled time, just hoping that somehow I could fit her in. With a full day, however, I gently asked her to return at her appointed hour the following week. "I trust it will be the perfect time," I assured her.

As she sat down across from me, I could see the spirit of her son joining us. He seemed relaxed, casual, and easygoing; the kind of guy who could just blend into the background, or go along with the crowd. Even the wrong crowd.

"Listen," said the woman. "I'm just going to lay this all out for you. You see, the police reports came back that his case was a clear example, an open-and-shut case of suicide. They claim he was even holding the weapon. But, I just don't think so. I think they just wanted to rush through it. I think they didn't want to deal with it. I think they're just too busy to know what's what. I know my son was struggling, and I know he purchased a gun. Still, I know he did not kill himself. So, I am asking you… Well, I am begging you… Please tell me my son did not commit suicide. Anything but suicide."

She cried and continued. "He doesn't even have to tell me the name of his killer. I am not going to prosecute. I just want him to say that he did not do this. I want him to tell me there is someone to blame. Maybe his money… Or they wanted his car. Please… not suicide!"

I felt such sadness for her, aching for the wounds she nursed and the shattered heart inside her. I prayed for serenity, for grace, and for the words to share. I could see, and her son confirmed, that he had ended his life, and I suspected she understood this, too. Yet, she could not endure the pain of knowing that he had done this. She could not live with his suicide.

Looking to her son, and trusting the wisdom within, I asked: "What would be different if he was murdered? He would still be physically absent? How would murder be different from suicide?"

She held her breath, then looked at me and cried bitterly: "Because if he committed suicide, it is my fault. I did not see it coming. If he killed himself, I will think that I killed him, because I did not stop him, I did not intervene. His death would be my fault if he committed suicide."

For several moments, I said nothing. I opened every corner and quieted every nook in my mind. I thought of only light and felt only love. No words could speak to this. I had to be with her in that moment. With all of my soul, I let myself be present. I let myself be.

After a few moments, I asked: "What if the reports are right and your thinking is slightly off base. What if he did commit suicide, but you're not to blame. What if you have no guilt?"

Then, for some time, I spoke to and for her son's spirit. He truly loved and cherished his mother and wanted only good for her. He found great strength in her smile and treasured memories of his upbringing. I confirmed many details for her, then relayed a powerful message from him.

"*My death had nothing to do with the life she gave me,*" said his spirit. "*My death, the physical end of me, was about turning over a new leaf, feeling renewed, and having a fresh start. I never blamed her, nor did I really consider her. I made my decision because I felt ready to let go, to be free, and to move on. Good or bad, the decision had nothing to do with her.*"

The death of those who commit suicide has nothing to do with the life that loved ones have given them. Life is a unique journey for each of us. And death most certainly is, too. What seems challenging to one soul may seem effortless to another. A tragedy to one may be a triumph to another. We all perceive life through a unique soul view. No one is all right, nor is anyone all wrong. As we perceive, so we become. Knowing this, we must accept that we are never to blame for the decisions of others. Nor are they at the cause for ours. We each choose our path, find our way, based on how we perceive, what we think we need, and why we believe we are here. Suicide is a no-fault death. There need be no one or nothing to blame.

Yet guilt persists. Those left behind after a suicide feel frozen, trapped, stuck.

From a spiritual perspective, the most powerful choice we can ever make in ending guilt in our lives it this: Trust.

When we surrender the need to control in exchange for a willingness to trust, we can find peace even in the midst of worldly uncertainty. Trust allows the mind to be still in times of chaos and the heart to be calm in the midst of unrest. When we make the choice to trust, we simultaneously affirm a higher wisdom and align with the possibility for revelation of a divine plan. Trust frees us from guilt, transcends the need for blame, and welcomes inspiration, creativity, and, most importantly, growth.

From a worldly perspective, suicide never makes sense. Those left behind may argue point counter point with reasons for the violent demise.

Before she left, the bereaved mother and I decided, with a little help from her son's spirit, to create an affirmation to help her neutralize guilt.

"I trust that he had his own good reasons, and this had nothing to do with me. I trust that I will honor my spirit today. I will find a way to live more peacefully. I trust."

In life after the death of those we love, we learn to hold on, to let go, to trust.

Although I wished for this mother a miracle cure, a magic potion, I realized that she had a long road to recovery ahead of her. Yet, in speaking with her son's spirit, in claiming a belief that she could learn to trust, I sensed the spell of denial had been broken and the shroud of perpetual darkness cast off. I trusted that she would have the strength to take a step forward. I surrendered the connection we had shared to love. I placed my heart in trust.

Later, after dinner, I began pondering the session and reflecting on the fragile nature of life. Clearly, making peace with a tragedy such as suicide takes tremendous determination, sheer desire, and unrelenting faith. When death is so apparent, undeniable, and seemingly final, it becomes easy to submit to guilt, difficult to learn to trust. I was to quicken my spiritual growth around this very concept in my own terms imminently.

My children and I sat in the living room; open and light, the south wall of the common area provides an abundant outdoor view with floor-to-ceiling windows. It was a cool evening in the late spring, when the weather can tease or please in a span of moments. I looked skyward and noticed dark clouds. I commented aloud, "It looks like it might storm."

My youngest daughter's eyes widened in panic. "Mommy, my tree!"

The prior year, when she was five, we decided to celebrate Earth Day by planting a tree together. Because she wanted to touch, love, and nurture her little tree, to have it close at hand, we purchased a small variety and placed it in a large pot. Our little tree received more tenderness than any tree I had ever known, and the unabandoningly wild love of a child proved a fertilizer divine: the little tree grew, blossomed, and thrived!

Noting the sky and gauging the proximity of the rain, I replied, "Let's get you in the tub. I have time to move the little tree." She smiled, relieved, and we activated the proposed plan.

While inside the tub filled with the strong flow of water, the clouds began to dump, to empty huge sheets of rain. Quickly, I stepped outside to move the little tree, and as I did, a violent gust of wind pushed against me. I nearly lost my footing but braced myself, with feet shoulder width apart; I then resumed my course. But at that moment, an enormously strong burst of wind forced a new course; the little tree, strong in its roots but vulnerable against the storm, snapped. I cried out then powered forward, pulling the heavy pot with all my might, fighting the elements, determined not to stop until the tree nestled close to the shelter of the house.

But it was too late. The fatal blow dealt, I could only clean up the damage. My stomach hurt, and my eyes stung. If only I had come out a moment sooner. If only I had known about the intensity of the storm. If only…

Trust.

In a timeless instant, I suddenly recalled the mother and her spirit son from the session. Like me, she did not realize the intensity of her son's storm, nor did she know how or precisely when to intervene. Like me, she saw her little sapling broken by the winds of change, the floods of emotions, storms.

Trust.

Wet and frazzled, cold and drained, I rushed to the bathroom to stop the water filling the tub. Though the experience seemed vast, only a minute or two had passed. My little girl busied herself with boats and bottlenose dolphins; bubbles filling the bath perched on the tip of her nose and gave sudsy streaks to her hair. She smiled at me as I leaned down, "Thanks, Mommy. Did you get the little tree?"

"Yes, sweetie, I did. I trust she's all right," came my honest reply.

For days the storms raged. As the tempestuous spring cleared, the sun shining again, we emerged from the house. The little tree had dropped a few leaves; those remaining browned. Though I had hoped that somehow the tree could repair its trunk and grow strong once more, this was not the path. Little tree could not endure.

We watched it for weeks, my daughter and I, hand in hand, giving our hearts to the rescue efforts. We sat with the tree, read books alongside the tree. Our love, though strong, would have to nurture the memories and grow the roots of goodness inside us.

One afternoon, acknowledging wordlessly between us the death of the tree, we decided to move the trunk, shift the soil, take stock. The miracle of trust, the gift of blind faith, the spirit of love, held fast by trust, proved to me that life finds a way and that always, always, love lives.

As I placed my hands in the soil, feeling the soft, moist dirt, I pushed aside some of the brown, fallen leaves. I discovered life… a few baby trees! Barely buds, too tiny to be saplings, the little springs found shelter, protection, and nutrients in the seeming lifeless tree. A family of rolypolies skittered by, and a few industrious ants busied themselves. New life! The lifeless tree embued its essence in the dawning of new life. Seeing this, recalling the message from the spirit son to his sorrowful mother, then seeing the incredible gift of eternal life and unconditional love, I felt deeply satisfied. Trust.

Similarly, I worked with a woman whose mother left a well-articulated, very eloquent suicide note. In the letter, penned on her best, monogrammed stationery, she explained difficulties with her work, a broken past with her father, and a struggle with an eating disorder which had starved her of all hope. She wanted out and believed it was her time to go home.

Her daughter argued with each explanation.

"I have had three jobs in the last two years and the company is downsizing now," she cried. "That's no reason to kill myself. And my dad barely speaks to me, except to tell me that I'm doing things wrong. Yeah, it's pretty rotten, but it's his loss. I'm not going to off myself. And please! Tell me about one person who feels good about their body. My mom was beautiful! Everyone loved her. I was trying to help her. I was doing all I knew to do. A hard life is no excuse for an easy death. These reasons are not good enough. I want my mom back!"

After speaking at length to her mother's spirit, confirming her presence, I allowed the bereaved daughter to hear the wisdom of her mother's spirit. She made a request of her daughter. "*Can you trust that I did what I felt I had to do? Can you trust that it may not have been easy for you, but it was mine to do? Can you trust?*"

I relayed this and spent some time with her daughter. If she trusted her mom, even though she did not understand or agree with her, she could begin to soften to her mother's presence and to ease with grace into her own healing. The cure for guilt is trust.

We cannot stop the storms of life from raging, for the rains will always come. But, we can ease our guilt with the power of trust. After suicide, we trust. Life finds a way. Love, timeless, enduring, eternal, will always live on. Trust.

CHAPTER 9

Forgive to Remember

GETTING SENT THROUGH THE DOOR to the right. Trapped in a dark place. Earthbound, lost, wandering. Just karmic fate.

Myths, misperceptions, and mistakes abound in the religious world and our culture about the soul, the afterlife, and suicide.

It is time to clear the air.

"So I had it coming, I guess. This lady told me that I had killed myself in a past life when he was my wife and I was the husband. So now, turnabout is fair play, at least with karma. I'm only reaping what I sowed in some other lifetime. I guess I had already sealed my fate."

The woman sitting with me sank into the chair and began to cry silently into her tissue. She was in her late 30s, petite, curly, dark blond hair, and big blue eyes. She invited trust with her sweet countenance and peace with her soft-spoken voice. I felt blessed to have the opportunity to assist her.

Clearly saddened by her loss, wanting to make some semblance of sense of an insane tragedy, she sought a psychic to help her sort herself out. Instead, she received a blow to her heart and a wound to her soul: she was, after all, to blame for her husband's death for her choice in a lifetime of which she had no recall, according to the other psychic's crystal ball.

She looked up at me again and asked: "Do you think that's true? That we just come back time and time again to be punished for our sins? Is it like a tag-you're it through eternity? So do I kill myself next time around? I guess I can live with it if it's fair, but it seems crappy to me." She finished her thought with a note of anger.

The concept of karma, which in the Hindu language simply means "action," has been through the westernized blender and become something completely new. Karma is seen as an eye for an eye, a part for a part, an action for an equal and opposite reaction by most of those who even care to consider the concept in our society. We throw the term around, and use it as a guise for manipulation or a paper-thin, pseudo-spiritual explanation for complex situations we don't readily understand... such as suicide.

My first exposure to the word karma was in college at a coffee shop, where gurus and junkies, philosophers and frat brothers converged for a common cause: sugary sweet, stimulating, sustaining caffeine, nectar for the sleep-deprived student's soul.

After ordering my tea, I happened to look down and see a tin can with a post-it note on the side. The handwritten message on the memo was: "Tips, please. Good karma!"

I cocked my head quizzically and asked the cashier, "What does this mean?" as I pointed to the can. We didn't talk about karma in the Baptist church.

"It means if you don't tip me, something bad will happen to you. But if you do, you'll have good luck," he answered with sincerity.

"Oh, that sounds like some sort of cosmic chain letter. If I break the chain, God's gonna send me bad luck?" I asked him, feeling suddenly uneasy.

"Hey, I didn't invent it. I'm just telling you what it is. If you don't like it, no problem. But still, will you tip me?" he almost begged.

As he presented my tea, feeling put on the spot, I begrudgingly dropped a few coins into the rattling can. He smiled and nodded, saying, "Now you'll have good luck."

I sat down thinking of this and wondering if I had, in fact, tipped my way to some kind of blessings. Had I bribed the Universe to be nice to me by offering a gratuity to this guy?

At that time, our country was experiencing a great deal of turmoil involving corporate corruption and high-level conspiracies fueled by greed. On a far-reaching scale, workers were discovering retirement accounts had been plundered and doctored so that CEOs and executives could enjoy excess, exotic lifestyles, and indulge in whatever they could want. Business leaders would take without asking and change without informing those individuals whom the change would affect. The rich got richer, and the poor stayed broke. No one seemed to mind.

Simultaneously, on the personal front, I had a dear friend battling ovarian cancer. A lovely woman, gracious and kind, she mothered five small children, to each of whom she was preparing to say goodbye. Nothing in me could imagine that she, in some past life, had done something bad to them or something harsh to anyone. I could not, in any way, imagine the she could ever be, in this life or any other, anything less than good. But this thing called karma had sealed her fate. In my mind, the spirit of grace and the concept of karma seemed to collide.

Curious about this new way of thinking, I began to explore the general concepts of karma, to observe how this tenet could fit into my newly emerging belief system, and to consider a new way of applying the teachings. With my fundamental Christian pillars crumbled after the suicide of my friend, I truly wanted to know more about the afterlife, but I was honestly scared to poke my nose in what I thought might not be any of my business.

The Bible seemed completely inaccessible and inapplicable to my life as a bereaved friend and young adult. The New Age movement, growing strong but secret, cloistered in back rooms of old bookshops, seemed a little too woo woo for me. I attended a Buddhist gathering and participated in numerous transcendental meditations. These were amazing, stirring experiences that brought me a tremendous experience of peace. But still, no answers or reconciliations with the afterlife.

In time, as I cultivated my skills as a medium and sought in every session a message of love and a spark of truth, I realized that karma does have an impact—but not the coffee shop teachings of which I was first told.

We are each responsible for creating and interpreting our experiences. Reality is really more accurately described as relativity. When we have certain thoughts and beliefs, we will somehow find ways to prove those things true in our lives. This is not about being good or bad, this is about the tenacious, exclusively human desire to be right.

As a child, I had a belief for many years that cats were the best kind of pet. I could find articles in magazines and health journals that proved this. I would share this information freely. One day, a friend of mine said: "I'm allergic to cats. They make me sick. I wonder why the best kind of pet could make me die?"

Not only was this a blow to my ego, but it jolted me into a new reality. Did the feline class suddenly change in its taxonomy or anatomy or physiology or behaviors? No. Did my own pet cat transform into a new breed? No. Did any single cat in the worlds' entirety alter itself in any way as a result of my personal, deflating revelation? Not at all. Only I had changed. Only me. I felt as if I had been proven wrong, that I was foolish. I suddenly saw my own cat as suspect.

This changed my actions, my karma. I felt a bit off. Not appreciating the conflict within me, I felt guilty for questioning my beliefs, for feeling a bit distant from my pet, and for having been so outspoken on something that seemed so inane. Interestingly, this intense desire to avoid the feeling of guilt caused me to start skipping lunch because my stomach hurt, and consequently I lost a bit of weight. I received the taunting nickname "String bean," and the moniker stuck on me for years. All because of a thought made destructive by my own sense of guilt.

Of course, in time I worked through this. I love my cats, frogs, tortoise, fish, and hermit crabs, too. But I don't have an attachment to one pet over another. Or any pet at all. I love what I love and trust others to find and choose what is best for them, too. I healed my personal pet karma and now enjoy the freedom to choose love for all.

So karma is not part for part, tit for tat. Karma is a process, an opportunity, really, where we experience our hidden beliefs made manifest in our lives, then have an opportunity to change. We can fool ourselves in our minds, keeping truth suppressed under justifications, hiding our light under bushels of guilt, pain, and darkness. But we are inevitable creators, unfailing manifestors of our thoughts. We will see what we believe. This is karma. It is not about God so much as it is about subtle perceptions and unclaimed emotions. And this is especially true with suicide.

Suicide is an individual decision, and for this choice no one is to blame. Suicide is not retribution, not a vengeance, not a penance to pay for deeds of lifetimes past. It is not a punishment, and most importantly, it is not an ending. A change, yes, but not an ending.

The woman whose husband had committed suicide was in no way to blame for his departure from the physical. Nor was this just the balancing of a scale, a "you hurt me/I hurt you" sort of payback. Not only was this a completely inaccurate interpretation, it set in motion the ongoing cycle of shame, blame, and suffering too often experienced by those left behind. Although past lives and patterns are certainly a consideration on a soul level when examining the greater reasons for suicide, we must not simply dismiss suicide to karma. No one had it coming. No one deserves to hurt.

In the end, the true motive behind suicide is a desire for freedom from emotional, mental, or physical dis-ease. When the pain is so great and the uncertainty is so engulfing, when the shakiness and instability of the landscape within collapses from beneath, when perception is dark to blinding, suicide provides a change in vision and a perspective that is new. When a suicide has happened, it is certain that it was the best cure.

The bereaved wife felt tremendous relief as we explored this thought, as we set free the fear of a karmic sentence, and as we spoke to the voice of her husband from beyond the body. He had found what he was looking for: a sense of ease and a moment of peace. In that instant, I could see that she sensed this, too.

On more than one occasion, I have heard about a "left door" and suicide. The first time this came to me, I worked with a woman whose best friend had ended her own life. In the wake, the bereaved friend sought a psychic to help her make sense of the death. She ended up confused and saddened by the information.

As we sat across from one another, she mentioned to me: "So, I was told that she went immediately through the left door and was shoved into a new body. She had to come back right away. It was her punishment for leaving; she had to come right back."

At that time, naïve to much of the pseudo-spiritual information about suicide out in the world, I had not heard of any "doors." I considered this for a moment, but decided my time would be best spent talking with the spirit of the young girl who had moved forward. This proved rewarding, educational, and healing indeed.

I believe the myths and misconceptions, the strange stories and dark mysteries that seem to abound in regards to the afterlife of those who commit suicide truly each come from a single place: fear. Historically, and even in contemporary times, any note of uncertainty, any element of fear will oftentimes elicit attempts to control and contain outcomes by conditioning through fear. Suicide is painful for those left behind, and the wounds seem, too often, unable to be healed. I believe that fear-based myths around suicide stem from a poorly implemented intention for suicide prevention...

But that is not the way. Not everyone who is riddled with depression, hollowed with sadness, swallowed up with anguish will hang on for more of the same. A soul willing to face uncertainty because the known reality is far too cruel is a soul that is suffering greatly, indeed. This suffering will not be met with further hurt. The afterlife is a place of healing and rest for all.

These myths and thinly veiled threats designed to keep those struggling here on Earth, here on Earth, backfire completely; for not only do these false teachings create a greater separation between physical existence and spiritual experience but the real victims are, once again, those who are left behind. This woman, told her friend had been shoved through some door, suffered because her friend was in such pain, then hearing about her friend's supposed outcome, hurt, ached, and suffered even more. Enough!

Incarnation is not a punishment. Nor is life in the physical, as hard as it often seems, designed to be some sort of cosmic cruel joke or karmic curse. We, powerful co-creators, choose to come here because we believe there is some good, some life, some way for us to grow toward our best interest and highest purpose. We come here to uncover our truth, to remember our connection, and to stretch, sometimes painfully, sometimes in a way that feels good. But we come here by choice. When we have sucked all the juices out of the nectar of life, we return home, healed, better for the journey, awakened to a deeper truth. This is inevitable for all.

As I spoke with the spirit of the young woman, the one who had committed suicide, she confirmed the power of free will and the unchangeable right to choose.

"I wanted to have some time to rest," she began. *"I needed to clear my head. After some time, I got a tour of the afterlife. I call it*

Heavenville. It's a busy place with much to do and lots to see. I kinda like to hang back. I met my grandpa who died before I was born and some of my guides, too. Every now and then, I think about coming back for another go. But I like it here. I'll wait until my time."

Her friend smiled, hearing these words. "Heavenville? Nice. And yes, she always did everything on her own sweet time. I love her. Nothing will change that. Will she have to come back into a bad situation to make up for all the pain she caused here?"

The question was fair. I put it to the spirit to whom I spoke.

"Part of my learning here is helping me understand what I could not quite accept there," she said. *"I always blamed myself for everyone else's problems. I shouldered the weight of the world. I thought if I were good enough, no one would have to struggle or suffer. Looking around, at all the problems, I could see evidence that I would never be strong enough. So I crumpled under the weight of my own burden, and I broke under the strain of my own despair. No one could have saved me. And I have come to understand that I cannot save anyone else.*

She concluded: *"So, I have to be in constant awareness that everyone touched by my death has a choice about what to do about it. I can't choose for them, and I can't fix them if they feel they're broken. No other person can, and we shouldn't expect that of anyone. We have to do our own work! The future life I live will reflect my level of understanding and acceptance of who I believe myself to be and what I think I deserve to receive. I am focused on seeing as much light as I can, so I can choose my next experiences wisely!"*

I learned so much that afternoon. I felt tremendously blessed.

Another common myth about suicide—one reported frequently, too—is that the soul of the deceased is lost is in a "dark place" or a purgatory and must be prayed out. Through my work, spanning over a decade of spirit contact with spirits who have transitioned by suicide, I will say that I can understand, to some extent, where this thought or myth may come from and how it may, at first glance, appear to be true. Yet, as we will explore, there is a value in the darkness and healing in a quiet place of rest.

Each and every soul, as we have explored previously, receives the same warm welcome and loving reception upon arrival on the Other Side. After the necessary time of acclimation, a deep, sustaining rest is granted. When we rest, we do so, in life and in the life beyond, in a darkened womb, warm and quiet, where we allow all our defenses to go down. We let go of all resistance, and we completely surrender into the wisdom, placing ourselves fully into the heart of a divine force called Love.

Sleeping in a well-lit room can be a challenge. Try falling asleep in the bright sunlight. The light invites activity, promotes expansion, enhances growth, grants acuity. When tired, weary from a long day's journey, a darkened room proves a perfect place to settle. The world is softer, quieter, more still in the dark. Night is a time of magic, mystery, spirit, and intuition. Much needed, necessary, the darkness gives contrast to the light.

This time of surrender, letting go, and complete freedom is vital to those who have committed suicide. One of the most beautiful explanations I have heard of this time came from a young man who had struggled with bipolar disorder for decades before he ended his physical presence through suicide.

"*I was tired. I was worn out. I was done,*" he said. "*My whole life I felt deformed even though my body looked fine. My heart hurt… all the time.*

"*When I returned to spirit, I could finally let go. And I did. I went into the most deep place, the darkest chamber that I imagine to be a like a womb. But not a physical place where a body is built. This was a womb of creation. As I released my mind into a quiet softness, I allowed my spirit to mend itself with inner wisdom. The divine, spiritual nature of me could have its beautiful course. I had dammed my heart, blocking out all good, and felt damned because of that. As I slept, the walls tumbled down, and the living waters of life healed me, washed me, cleansed me 'til I remembered I was whole. This woke me up! Something started percolating in me, and I stirred, then roused from my slumber. I had risen indeed.*

"*I love my family, but please tell them that I did not need prayed out of that place! Why wake a beautiful, sleeping child who is tucked in safely for slumber? My mother will remember watching me sleep and what a deep sense of peace that gave her. She knew that if I made it safe through the day, if I could sleep so soundly at night, as I lay so soft and still, everything in the world, for that fleeting moment as she would look at me in slumber, was all right. That was Heaven experienced on Earth. Everything is all right.*"

He explained: "*Don't wake a peacefully resting spirit! No need to jostle me with fearful pleadings and prayers. Let me be and only love me. Only love!*"

His sister, the client who I served, began to cry. "Did the prayers hurt him?"

He quickly replied: "*Prayers cannot wound. But the fear that drives the prayers does. Do not fear for those who are physically gone, for we are always living. We live as spirit and we dwell in light. Pray for peace to feel this and pray for openness of mind to trust and accept this. Pray for strength to continue on your own path. But do not pray me out! Connect with me, honor me, for I am whole, free, living my life.*"

A death by suicide is not an end. It is simply a rebirth, an opportunity for all, those passed and those left behind, to find a deeper appreciation for the vast journey, the eternal spirit, that we call life.

CHAPTER 10

Floating Boats
and Driftwood

WE LIVE IN A WORLD where image seems to be everything and smart style reigns as king. Facebook and social media encourage taking life literally at face value; we are trained to react instantly and with intensity to what we see.

Especially when you're 13.

I placed the call to the Southwest to a woman awaiting me. Though I looked outside to a cold, snowy white background, she, parched by a desert sun, had dressed herself in shorts and a t-shirt that day. I knew this because her daughter's spirit excitedly chattered at me before her mom so much as picked up the phone.

"*Mom's wearing my shirt. I want you to tell her that I see it,*" spoke the girl's spirit. "*She kept them all. She and the family had shirts made in my name after I died. Tell her I know that, too. I appreciate all she does in my honor and in my memory. She even has my hairbrush. Please tell her she blesses me every day and all the time.*"

"Hello," her mother answered at the other end.

I took a deep breath and eased into the conversation. Though pleasant, the mother's desperation to connect with her daughter's spirit felt palpable over the phone. She confirmed this by asking directly, "So will you tell me what my little angel has to say. I can't wait. Not another minute."

Permission fully granted, access to the realm of spirit gained, I began a beautiful exchange, a conversation that danced with Heaven and Earth. The daughter's spirit laughed about disastrous birthday parties of days in the past, joked over burned pizza and fireworks, mood rings, earrings, class rings, and onion rings. There was no doubt to me, or her mother, that her spirit lived on

Her spirit spoke. "*I was scared. Really scared. I didn't know what anyone would think of me. I didn't want me or her or our family to look bad. I am sorry. I was scared.*"

I expressed these messages to her mom as this 13-year-old's story unraveled before me. As a seventh-grader learning to fit into the popular crowd, she struggled to find her place in life. Though she was the oldest of five children, she seemed to walk between two worlds: very mature, responsible, dutiful, she spoke and related to adults well; light-hearted, childish, and innocent of heart, she blended well with preschoolers, too. Yet she longed to experience acceptance in a group of her own kind. She wanted friends.

In junior high, she made the dance team. This marked a new beginning for her, as she spent time with peers. Her skills sharp, her desire high, she practiced daily and felt proud. Her family expressed tremendous pride in her accomplishment, too.

Then, one afternoon, at practice, she botched the routine. Harsh criticism ensued, and she left in tears. From the place of emotional devastation, fearing she would never recover, hating herself and lacking belief that she could ever heal, she locked herself in her parents' bedroom and ended the fear with a single shot from a gun. No note, no goodbye. Gone.

The family, shaken to the core, reeled in the trauma and ached in her loss. The youngest siblings, ages three, five, and six, repeatedly asked her to come home so that together they could watch for the rain.

Making note of this, the girl's gentle spirit commented: "*I miss the rain. But I will always be there to watch them float the boats.*"

Initially the message didn't make much sense to me, yet I communicated her words: "*Float the boats…*"

The message elicited audible sobs from her mom. "Oh, every

108

time it rains! She and the boys would go outside in the storms, splashing and stomping in the rain, and let little stick boats float down the rushing waters of the drainage ditch. Our house is on a hill, so the downpours offer a perfect waterway for homemade watercraft. But last week, for the first time since her death, we went out in the downpour and released some boats. My goodness how I cried as the boats floated out of sight. I just wanted her to be there. She was the one who should be floating the boats, not me!"

Her mother's sadness seemed to intensify for a moment, as she relived the memory of seeing the boats slip away. Her too-young-to-die daughter's life had seemed to slipped away, too.

"I want her back. How can I hold her or see her one more time? I just want to feel her and know she's okay," her mom begged.

Her daughter's response was poignant, pure. "*Keep talking to me, Mom. Don't fight the tears. And when it rains, go outside. Float the boats.*"

Separation through physical death, and especially through suicide, stretches us to our human limits and exposes our vulnerability. Nonlinear, nonsequential, sometimes nonsensical, the grief process can leave us feeling emotionally raw. We long for one more touch, one more hug, one more kiss.

Yet, if we are willing, we can experience connection to those in spirit through physical means. Cultivating and practicing meaningful, thoughtful, and conscious rituals and ceremonies provides comfort, emotional release, peace.

In esoteric traditions, four elements give rise to the fragile strong miracle of physical life. Meaningful ceremonies can incorporate each of these elements in some way to become deeply satisfying and highly sacred. By tapping into the primal forces and essential drives of our earthly beings, we can maintain strong bonds with those who have passed on.

The first element is fire. Fire gives rise to our passions, our actions, our instincts; it is the ember that burns at the very core of who we are. Fire is a protector, an illuminator, a place of gathering where we encircle one another in community. Fire ignites, and we release. We find the clarity to stay strong.

Lighting candles offers an easy yet powerful way to honor those who have moved on and stoke the fires that cannot be snuffed by physical death. A simple votive candle placed on a table and lit with intention can provide immense comfort without pretense. Lighting candles at birthdays, anniversaries, milestones, significant life moments affirms the inextinguishable bond that we share with deceased loved ones. Placing a picture of those who have moved on near the flame constitutes a powerful ceremony, indeed

The next element is water. Allowing this force of nature to flow through our rituals and ceremonies renews, cleanses, and washes pure the heart desiccated with grief. Water conducts energy quickly and efficiently, serving as a natural medium for release of pent-up, stagnant, unhealthy emotions. We are creatures of water, formed in the secret, dark, primordial womb of life.

The beach, a river, a lake, a small pond, even a bath drawn with intention—all invite a spiritual connection and release. Journaling by the ocean's edge, praying on the shore, or soaking submerged in the warmth of water constitute ritual.

"I had to do it. I went on the cruise. Just as we planned. I took his ashes, too," the young woman shared with me, as I spoke with her husband's spirit. "Our plan was to go together, but his depression got the best of him. But he was with me. His remains and his spirit. I knew that he would be with me, if he could, somehow."

Her husband, a brilliant man with tremendous talent, ambition, and drive, had for many years struggled with severe depression behind closed doors. Compounding his feelings was guilt over these

110

feelings. He struggled, believing he shouldn't feel the way he felt, adding insult to injury. Psychically fractured, he sought professional help and received numerous medications to combat the darkness that loomed.

Yet the medicines only numbed him, and the battle raged on, until he became too tattered and torn to fight. Just days before his birthday, and only a week prior to their departure for a cruise, he committed suicide.

"*But it all makes sense,*" his spirit explained. "*I can accept who I am. And I know that I was not the jobs that I did. My vision was so scattered, shattered, messed up. I could never have seen that in my lifetime. Please tell my wife that she will find love. She can move on. She has to! There is more in store for her. When she was on the water, for the cruise, please let her know that I sent the dolphins. It was the least I could do.*"

I relayed this message. His wife heaved a sigh. "I knew it. I knew," the words flowed through her.

Moments after she released his ashes from the deck, a pod of dolphins began leaping and playing near the ship. Though her ceremony was simple, the effects were powerful. She knew that he was well, that his essence waltzed with dolphins. The sea provided a perfect setting for an eternal moment of Heaven and Earth as one.

Water renews.

The third element to include in sacred ritual and spirit connections is air. Air represents communication, expression, inspiration, intellect, and information received mentally through insight. Inclusion of this element in mindful spiritual practices will foster the ability to glean deeper understanding into the nature of life and death, to understand from a broader perspective the anatomy of soul, and to expand the consciousness of past, present, and future life contracts.

The air element vivifies music, rhythm, and song. The blending of voices in a harmony can only be appreciated through the vibration of sound carried lovingly through the air. Music is a frequent messenger for spirit and for those who have passed on.

"She always plays it for me. It's uncanny," stated my client, as I mentioned her mother's spirit sang "Amazing Grace" for me.

Her mother suffered a degenerative brain disease and feared becoming a burden on the family. Dignified, brought up in a religious home, she raised her own children to respect God. Her favorite song, which she often hummed while making dinner, was the old hymn, "Amazing Grace."

As her disease progressed, she worried that she would lose control, be somehow stripped of her dignity. Not able or willing to face that, she ended her life while she was reasonably strong. Though her family felt frustration and tremendous grief, her surviving daughter understood her mother's choice. She respected her mother's grace and dignity.

A few weeks after her mom's transition, the daughter began a nightly ritual of lighting a candle. Often she would do this just before turning off the TV. On the first night of her candlelight vigil, the sound of "Amazing Grace" hit the air as her daughter turned the TV off.

The next night, after lighting the candle, the daughter made her way to the television, taking notice when the lead character on the broadcast show mentioned a fictional friend named Grace. A few nights later, after lighting the candle, she heard a preview for the "Amazing Race" TV show.

On and on, in highly creative ways, the song would be played or alluded to. The daughter suspected this was her beloved mother's handiwork. My messages from her spirit confirmed this.

Air can be represented with feathers, wind chimes, music, or clouds. Air inspires.

The last element vital for spirit connections and integral for the creation of sacred ritual is earth. Nature, the physical world into which we are born, grow, and to which we return when our journey is through, offers timeless lessons of seasons and cycles, trust, non-resistance, adaptation, surrender, and presence. Our earth shapes, reshapes, expands, contracts, spins, creates, reuses, invents, flexes, moves endlessly through space and time. Earth does not question; it simply lives. This element represents strength, trust, and growth.

The same rains that wash the lands now washed the scales and tails of dinosaurs. The atoms of the rotten leaf, fallen on the grass-carpeted forest floor, are gifted to a berry bush, which grows fresh fruit that nourishes fledgling baby birds. The elements and compounds of our earthy bodies have been here since our planets fiery hot, passionate birth from a mother star exploding our solar system into being with her fatal labor pains millions of years ago. Our ancestors are not just connected through DNA; we are physically built from their stuff. In truth, there is no separation.

So when a loved one dies by suicide, the earth receives and reenergizes the cells to life, brand new. Though the body cannot return as it once was, the atoms, molecules, compounds are surely reinfused with purpose. No life, no substance, nothing is ever wasted.

The physical effects of those we have lost serve as a symbol of earth element. From teddy bears to t-shirts, trinkets to treasures, the personal property left behind often serves as a vital tool for connection.

I worked with a woman whose son had ended his physical life after a string of bad luck. Leaving a note, he drove his car off a steep embankment. During the young man's childhood, his parents divorced and his mother remarried, to a very humble, kind man. The stepfather served as a gentle, consistent, trusted mentor for the often troubled but good-hearted young man.

As I began communicating with the spirit of the affable youth, I understood that he had much unexpressed love and appreciation for the stepfather; their bond was strong and the feelings deep. The young man's spirit showed me a bottle of cologne, and asked that I tell his stepdad I could see and smell the scent of it.

Upon hearing the message, the stepfather dropped his head into his hands. Though he had never told anyone, not even his beloved wife, he kept a bottle of his stepson's cologne back as the family cleared out some of the young man's toiletries. He tucked the cologne in the back of his closet, in a shoebox, and from time to time, when he felt overwhelmed or swallowed up with grief, he would open the bottle for a whiff; just a spray was enough for him to remember the connection the two shared.

His stepfather stated: "Only a small amount, and only once in a while, and I remember the love we shared. We didn't talk about it much, or label it, or analyze it. We just knew we had something. Knowing that was enough. When I smell his cologne, I remember what I knew. I appreciate that I was able to be there for him. I loved him. I think I always will."

His stepson's spirit quickly spoke. *"What we share is eternal, not a thing of the past. Our bond cannot be severed, and that love cannot die. I love you. I always will."*

Connecting with the earth element allows us to physically connect with the stuff and substance of those who have moved on. From stones to stuffed animals, these symbols are vital to mindful, meaningful ceremony and ritual.

Earth strengthens.

An example of one on the most beautiful, thoughtful ongoing ceremonies I have witnessed happened between a mother and her son's spirit. Her son, at age 17, committed suicide. As the session unfolded, blossoming like a rose coming into full bloom, I marveled at the power of love and the presence of spirit, washed ashore as driftwood.

The two lived near the beach. The young man wrestled with fitting in, with relationships with girls, with school, with his estranged father. Like all teens, he felt extremes in his life and often grappled with how to hold on and when to let go.

Yet, as he neared graduation, the fears and insecurities seemed to amplify and intensify, he wondered if he could find a job, a place; he questioned that he could live on his own. He looked to his father, a ghost of a parent. Just before his graduation, the father denounced him, delivering the irrecoverable blow.

Three days before commencement, he committed suicide.

As I spoke with his spirit, I could see a long, glorious stretch of beach, honey-golden sand glowing against the pink and copper hues of an etheric sunset. The waves lapped playfully in and out, tousling the shoreline. Then, I could see his spirit holding a unique piece of driftwood. "*Tell my mom I send them for her.*"

Relaying this vision to her, I delivered the message. Her voice leapt with excitement. "I knew it! I knew it was him. I knew it. Thank you!"

Shortly after he ended his physical life, she began taking sunset walks along the beach. One evening, on the heels of a particularly emotional day, she noticed a piece of driftwood; the color and shape of it caught her eye: white and wispy, it looked almost like a feather.

She took the driftwood home and laid it aside.

Days later, she noticed another similar hunk of driftwood. Again, she took the floating treasure home and set it aside.

With every seaside stroll, a strikingly beautiful and wonderfully original offering would present itself to her. Amassing so many pieces, she decided to assemble them in random fashion. Completing an afternoon of work, she stood back to take in the fruits of her labor.

To her amazement, she noticed the assemblage had taken form as a driftwood, salt-kissed angel.

The daily sea stroll became a sacred unfurling of divine expression: what appeared dead, the driftwood, took on life anew in the shape and size of an angel.

"This touches me, it gives me hope. I know he is guiding me and with me still. He had to move on, I can accept that to some extent. But I am so glad to know that he can see me, that he can help me, that he loves me still. I will keep walking if he will keep sending the driftwood to me. I love you, son!" she remarked, happily.

The sacred ritual of the seaside walk invited Heaven to pour forth as Earth. The merging of the earth at the water's edge, with the fiery sun setting in the cool mists of evening air provided a perfect place for the union of two souls, together for a time as mother and son, but connected endlessly through a divine loveline.

Honoring those who have committed suicide with mindful and conscious ceremony, ritual, and celebration offers a human, tangible, palpable way to bridge the gap between the physical absence and spiritual presence. Utilizing fire, earth, air, and water brings the full force of nature into harmony with the spark of life. As we grieve, we release and renew. Love heals.

CHAPTER 11

Bridging The Gap

FEELING READY TO TAKE ON THE WORLD, or at least my little corner of it, I decided, at the tender age of 16, to apply for my first part-time job. Still a student and desiring only a small income, I pursued employment at a fast food establishment close to home. The perks included half-price biscuits, the hourly minimum wage of $4.25, one 15-minute break per shift, and unlimited soft drinks while on duty. After an interview with a student-friendly manager, I was readily offered a position. I accepted gladly.

I cashed my first paycheck at the local grocery store, where my family was known. I did this for the second payroll, too. Having cash to stash felt powerful for a teenage girl. Yet I realized that keeping my assets tucked under the mattress or stuffed into a sock drawer was not the most clever way to build a successful financial portfolio. After talking with a trusted family and friend, I chose to open a checking account.

In addition to starter checks and a navy blue plastic checkbook cover that was gold embossed with the bank's logo, the account agent presented me with a ledger. In this booklet I was to keep track of my deposits and withdrawals. In any moment, I would know exactly how much money I had at my disposal.

Every month, near the end, I would receive a statement. The statement, printed on green-and-white paper, documented exactly how much of my money flowed through the bank's computer. I would compare my ledger with the bank's statement and reconcile the two. Most often, the documents would match. If not, I would have refiguring to do. This was a vital part of my wise money management. If I miscalculated and overspent, extra fees could be incurred. On the other hand, I wanted to fully credit myself with all the money that was my due. Only through reconciliation could I make sure my calculations and the bank's numbers would coincide.

Some months, reconciling the statement felt cumbersome, a bit like a chore. But the experience brought me a greater awareness about my values and desires. For example, one month I realized that I had spent a large amount of money on specialty teas. I made a decision to scale back on this practice. Another month, my book budget nearly broke the bank, but I chose to spend more than I ordinarily would for a collection of my favorite author's books.

I valued the process and stuck with it, even when it was hard, because I could learn and then choose how to use my financial resources. I did my best not to criticize and judge how I spent or what I spent my money on. Instead, I focused on empowering myself with knowledge and activated my ability to make conscious choices.

Imagine, then, that deciding to incarnate is a bit like opening a checking account. While in the realm of Spirit, dwelling on the Other Side, we, learning across space and time, build up enough desire and wisdom to put our resources into one tool: a body. We talk with some trusted spirit helpers and angel guides and agree to a mission, a soul plan. Incarnation, then, is a series of energetic deposits and withdrawals that affect the body, the emotions, and the life that we choose. In time, through death, we close the account and reconcile the experiences of our soul: the life review.

Bypassing the life review may seem tempting for those who have committed suicide. Why look back at a life that was willingly and readily ended? But without the experience of observing habits, understanding patterns, and becoming aware of areas of excess or behaviors that are skewed, the chance to change those very undermining and limiting choices is lost. Unconsciously, but out of habit, the soul will incarnate with unfinished business and can feel dissatisfied, paralyzed, or frozen in overwhelming, niggling feelings that interfere with choosing for the greater good.

We are by our very nature emotional beings. From conception to death, we feel vibrations, emotions, intentions to our very core. Vitally, intrinsically, our humanity stirs us, rouses us, and can either stunt us or inspire us to grow. Our emotions are complex, to be sure, and herein lies one of the greatest mysteries and most wondrous gifts of the journey we take in this world.

As a society, and in our culture, emotions are often disregarded, mocked, misunderstood, or used against us. A distant second to intellect, emotions are perceived as weakness or lack of control. Yet, through media and movies, we watch grandiose, extreme feelings and passions revered and highly romanticized. We live our emotions through characters, exacting vengeance, expressing forbidden lusts and hidden passions, acting on secret desires and wishes. We begin to believe that we should feel certain ways, we should not feel other ways, that we ought to feel good all the time, and if we don't, then something is terribly, horribly wrong with us.

We hold inside us the secret, terrifying fear that we *are* our emotions. Rather than *feeling* anger, we *become* anger. We can't simply *feel* guilty; we *are* guilty. Passing waves of sadness become the framework for our ongoing identity. . . we don't just *feel* sad; we *are* sad.

Emotions are not expressions of our identity; emotions, from a true, spiritual perspective, indicate where we stand in relationship to our soul. Feeling anger indicates choices, expectations, and behaviors that have diverted us from our true nature. Feeling good indicates that we are behaving and believing in a way that is aligned with our best and brightest self. Emotions are tools for empowerment and self-realization that inspire us to choose and use our personal truth.

So often, those who commit suicide have a lifetime's worth of unexperienced, unprocessed, unexpressed, and misunderstood emotions. The inability to recognize and utilize these powerful indicators bottlenecks growth and stifles the ability to find peace and harmony with the journey of life. Feeling overwhelmed with emotions often has a downward spiral effect for those who struggle, slip into depression, and sometimes commit suicide. Those who face such darkness too often cannot find the light.

The life review is the light at the end of the tunnel. Emotional liberation, freedom from darkness, a triumphant call to understand and embrace fully the choices made during incarnation mean that the soul's greatness is unleashed in the uncompromising presence of compassion and the unfathomable spirit of unconditional love. When we trust that we are truly loved, completely understood, and warmly received, we are free. This is the gift of the review.

As discussed, the life review is no final judgment. It is not a sentencing, and no punishment is doled out for our supposed sins. Instead, the life review is a powerful and sacred rite of passage where we as souls are given the chance to feel our emotions, to deeply profoundly experience the effects of our choices, and to go deep within the mind and heart to a place that is peaceful and still, where we can find rest, make peace, and be complete with the life that has been lived. The liberation, the freedom, the abiding peace that springs forth from the life review process is extraordinary.

Spirit guides, family who have preceded us in death, pets, and guardian angels stay by our side as we watch the life review. Without judging, simply loving, their presence encourages us to let go of the pain and suffering in exchange for healing and ease. In some traditions, the life review is described as a panoramic view of life; others detail a theater much like a place where we view a blockbuster film. Regardless, the life review allows us to feel, heal, cleanse, and renew.

Those who commit suicide, nearly always rife with guilt and racked with anger, outrage, or ill will, hesitate to participate in the life review, fearing sentencing, reprimand, or punitive action. For some souls, the review process starts but is not finished; the emotions become too intense to reexperience or move through. Not an all-or-nothing process, the life review can be partially undertaken then abandoned, or not partaken at all. Free will, self-determination, reigns supreme.

The life review can also take place, in part, while still occupying a physical body.

"He shot himself but was comatose for three months before we took him off life support," the middle-aged woman confirmed to me, as I spoke with her and the spirit of her nephew, who had committed suicide. "I was there with the family as the tubes were removed. At first, the entire room felt cold and vacant. Then. I don't know… "

She trailed off and fell silent for a moment.

"Something changed. For a moment he seemed to smile, then suddenly flatline. He was gone," she explained. "Will you ask him what happened?"

Glad to oblige, his spirit explained: "*As my body lay in that hospital bed, I was in limbo. I felt stuck. I did not want to go back to my body, but I was too scared to look at what might lie beyond. I could sense my grandfather's spirit around me. He died when I was a kid. But I just couldn't budge. Too much fear.*

"*But, in time, I could see my grandpa,*" he expressed. "*I also sensed our dog, who had died years ago. I saw my friend from high school who had drowned. Something in me decided to take a step forward. That was when my family felt at peace with pulling the plug. As I unstitched from my body, like untethering a line, I looked up and saw light. Well, I ran past it, looking only briefly as I saw a few glimpses and took a little glance. But then I stepped into this Other World, and I felt home."*

Something struck me as he spoke. At the very moment he experienced the spiritual readiness to step out of the shadows of fear and into the realm of light and the unknown, his family experienced spiritual readiness to release his body. Connected through love, and communicating soul to soul, the man and his family aligned in letting his body go. The timing was impeccable and orchestrated by divine design.

This is always the case. We are clued in, cued up, to the desires and needs of our loved ones as they prepare to release the body and step into the light. Through dreams, powerful feelings, unexplained knowing, and strong urges, we receive these messages just in time. Situations coalesce and circumstances converge not by accident or happenstance, but by the alignment and synchronization of minds.

"From the day he was born I knew I would not have much time with him," said the mother of a 20-year-old man who had taken his life. "He didn't leave a note and wasn't exhibiting any of the usual symptoms of someone who was suicidal. So when the police showed up to tell me of his death by suicide, I was devastated but not really surprised. For the first time since his birth, those unshakable feelings I tried to hide from made sense."

His spirit, speaking to me softly, confirmed this.

"It wasn't inevitable. I didn't have to commit suicide. It wasn't my fate. But my soul, and my mom's soul, too, knew that it was a strong and viable option. We were both, in some way, prepared. The night I committed suicide, I felt such ache and pain and a huge relief and surge of light that I could not go back. I had to go on."

Yet, like the man who lay comatose, this spirit participated in a partial life review before entering deep soul rest.

"I didn't really want to look," he went on. *"I never even looked at pictures or home movies of myself on Earth. Why would I look at my life and death! I experienced enough to understand that I was home, that my decision about suicide was not judged, then that was enough! I was through!"*

Enough? Perhaps. But perhaps not.

At that moment during the session, I experienced a turning point in my career, when the young man explained: *"We're One Mind, you know. Mom knew this. She can help us both. She can write a review for me! Then she will feel peace, and I will see more clearly."*

A deep sense of clarity and calm washed over me, as his spirit offered this guidance. His mother must have sensed this, too, because she responded nearly instantly, saying: "Okay! I will absolutely do it. How?"

Over the course of the next 20 minutes, I found myself receiving a truly "higher" education, as the wise soul led me through the process. Simple, elegant, powerful, effective, and, most importantly deeply healing, the life review works because we are all connected through one mind, one spirit, one Source. By reviewing, with compassion and love, the earthly walk of another, we heal ourselves and those on the Other Side, too.

The life review is a perspective, a narrative. Dates, times, titles matter not. The purpose of the tool is to seek and find the moments of connection and the touch points with Love that move us from one season of life to the next. But even more, the life review allows a sacred space to feel that which was unexpressed, and to release the emotions too deeply buried to be revealed in the physical world. There is no judgment in the life review—only a release from the darkness and a return to Love.

The young man's spirit, a teacher extraordinaire, said: *"Mom can talk about how I acted as a child. How I connected to those I loved, and how those I loved connected with me. She can write about my triumphs, my tragedies, my turning points. Tell her to write it all! Nothing need be held back. I'm not afraid now. Fear can't stop me or hold me back. This will help her! We can both feel free from the pain of my life and the sadness of my death. It's time!"*

As she left my office, the mother expressed excitement, satisfaction, deep peace, and a bit of intimidation. "I'm not a writer," she said. "But if it's good for him, I will do it!"

The life review, the manuscript, whether typed or handwritten, can be discarded, saved, burned, or simply put aside. There is no right or wrong way to use the document. The healing comes in the process of writing, in the feeling of the emotions, in the clarity and insight gained through the exercise. Rather than being contingent on the result, it is in the process that grace is claimed and the spirit of freedom powerfully moves. The soul, believed lost, is found. The blinded, bereaved family or friend will once again see!

From out of the darkness, stepping into the light, the life review renews.

CHAPTER 12

After the Rain

THIS IS NOT THE END. Though the words come slowly now, the messages complete, the final chapter nearly through, death is not the end.

Perhaps the greatest gift gained on the other side of suicide, when we face the deepest, most bitter darkness, is finding and tasting the sweetness of light. To understand that Spirit is a constant presence that transcends all physical comforts beyond measure. To know that the ties of love we share can never be broken or unbound by human constraints profoundly pacifies the restless heart. Love simply cannot, will not die.

Those who commit suicide are unfettered, untethered, unencumbered in every way. The love that awaits them in the light completely soothes the shattered heart and mends the wounded soul.

But that same light is here now.

We must train ourselves, teach ourselves, re-mind ourselves with each breath that Heaven—Peace, Paradise—is not a faroff place, a distant space where cherubs frolic on fluffy clouds. The Love of Spirit, the presence of Source, is not somewhere out there. We need not experience physical death to access what awaits us beyond.

Peace, Love, Heaven, Paradise, or whatever you wish to call it, is within, tucked in the heart, held in the still part of the mind.

Love is the silence behind the noise, the light beyond the darkness, the sun that shines above the clouds, even on a rainy, gray day. Love is the tie that binds us without labels, the force that connects us beyond words. It is on the highways and byways, the backstreets and side streets, written across the bathroom walls. Love is the moments, the breaths, the tears we shed and the laughter that echoes in the memories of our hearts and the notions in our head.

Love is.

Those left behind by suicide can heal. By resting in blessed assurance that those lost are found, by creating meaningful rituals and celebrations, by writing and rewriting a life review, by opening and accessing supportive, simple spiritual communion with those who have moved on, we heal.

Grief exposes the tender underside of the human soul, so often hidden by a hard protective shell from the world. As we move through loss, saturated in the raw emotions, we come to know just how fragile we are, how uncertain the journey, how changeable the course. In an instant, worlds collide, mountains crumble, and the face so familiar is forever gone.

But not lost.

Grief is a process and a journey. It comes in waves.

To believe there is an impetuous, passionate, singular rendezvous with grief is wrong. To think that death turns grief on, then a prayer or meditation turns it off (*Poof, it's gone*) is a fallacy. There is no technique that is the one. Healing is not one time; it's one more time… time and time again.

But, empowered by Spirit, steeped in compassion, choosing forgiveness, holding on, letting go, we can hope, we can smile, we can live again.

We face the darkness and breathe, clinging to moments, struggling, scraping by, scarcely dreaming until we find the light.

On the other side of suicide is light. Look!

Let it shine.

F I N D H O R N   P R E S S

Life-Changing Books

Consult our catalogue online
(with secure order facility) on
www.findhornpress.com

For information on the Findhorn Foundation:
www.findhorn.org

green press
INITIATIVE

Findhorn Press is committed to preserving ancient forests and natural resources. We elected to print this title on 30% post consumer recycled paper, processed chlorine free. As a result, for this printing, we have saved:

9 Trees (40' tall and 6-8" diameter)
4 Million BTUs of Total Energy
798 Pounds of Greenhouse Gases
4,325 Gallons of Wastewater
290 Pounds of Solid Waste

Findhorn Press made this paper choice because our printer, Thomson-Shore, Inc., is a member of Green Press Initiative, a nonprofit program dedicated to supporting authors, publishers, and suppliers in their efforts to reduce their use of fiber obtained from endangered forests.

For more information, visit www.greenpressinitiative.org

Environmental impact estimates were made using the Environmental Defense Paper Calculator. For more information visit: www.papercalculator.org.

MIX
Paper from
responsible sources

FSC
www.fsc.org
FSC® C013483